Andrew Green

Series Editor: Marian Cox

High Windows

Philip Larkin

Philip Allan Updates
Market Place
Deddington
Oxfordshire
OX15 0SE
Tel: 01869 338652
Fax: 01869 337590
e-mail: sales@philipallan.co.uk
www.philipallan.co.uk

ISBN-13: 978-1-84489-214-3
ISBN-10: 1-84489-214-X

Printed by MPG Books, Bodmin

Environmental information
The paper on which this title is printed is sourced from mills using wood from managed, sustainable forests.

Contents

Introduction

Aims of the guide

The purpose of this Student Text Guide to Philip Larkin's *High Windows* is to enable you to organise your thoughts and responses to the poems, to deepen your understanding of their key features and aspects, and to help you to address the particular requirements of examination questions in order to obtain the best possible grade. The edition of *High Windows* used in preparing this guide is the one published by Faber and Faber in 1974. Reference is also made to *The Whitsun Weddings* (Faber and Faber, 1964), to the *Collected Poems of Philip Larkin*, edited by Anthony Thwaite (Faber and Faber, 1988), and to *Required Writing: Miscellaneous Pieces 1955–82* (Faber and Faber, 1983).

It is assumed that you have read and studied *High Windows* already under the guidance of a teacher or lecturer. This is a revision guide, not an introduction, although some of its content provides background information and analysis of particular poems. It can be read in its entirety in one sitting, or it can be dipped into and used as a reference guide to specific and separate aspects of the poems.

The remainder of this Introduction consists of an outline of the Assessment Objectives; revision advice; and guidance on writing examination essays.

The Text Guidance section consists of a series of subsections which examine key aspects of the poetry including contexts, themes, imagery and analysis of specific poems. Emboldened terms within the Text Guidance section are glossed in 'literary terms and concepts' (pp. 68–70).

The final section, Questions and Answers, provides examples of essay titles, essay plans and examination essays, along with advice on how to make use of criticism on Larkin in your own writing.

Assessment Objectives

The Assessment Objectives (AOs) for A-level English Literature are common to all boards:

AO1	communicate clearly the knowledge, understanding and insight appropriate to literary study, using appropriate terminology and accurate and coherent written expression
AO2i	respond with knowledge and understanding to literary texts of different types and periods

AO2ii	respond with knowledge and understanding to literary texts of different types and periods, exploring and commenting on relationships and comparisons between literary texts
AO3	show detailed understanding of the ways in which writers' choices of form, structure and language shape meanings
AO4	articulate independent opinions and judgements, informed by different interpretations of literary texts by other readers
AO5i	show understanding of the contexts in which literary texts are written and understood
AO5ii	evaluate the significance of cultural, historical and other contextual influences on literary texts and study

This can be summarised as:

AO1	clarity of written communication
AO2	informed personal response in relation to time and genre (literary context)
AO3	the creative literary process (context of writing)
AO4	critical and interpretative response (context of reading)
AO5	evaluation of influences (cultural context)

It is essential that you pay close attention to the AOs, and their weighting, for the board for which you are entered. These are what the examiner will be looking for, and you must address them *directly* and *specifically*, in addition to proving general familiarity with and understanding of the text, and being able to present an argument clearly, relevantly and convincingly.

Remember that the examiners are seeking above all else evidence of an *informed personal response* to the text. A revision guide such as this can help you to understand the text and to form your own opinions, but it cannot replace your own ideas and responses as an individual reader.

Revision advice

For the examined units it is possible that either brief or more extensive revision will be necessary because the original study of the text took place some time previously. It is therefore useful to know how to go about revising and which tried and tested methods are considered the most successful for literature exams at all levels, from GCSE to degree finals.

Below is a guide on how not to do it — think of reasons why not in each case. **Don't**:

- leave it until the last minute
- assume you remember the text well enough and don't need to revise at all
- spend hours designing a beautiful revision schedule
- revise more than one text at the same time
- think you don't need to revise because it is an open book exam
- decide in advance what you think the questions will be and revise only for those
- try to memorise particular essay plans
- reread texts randomly and aimlessly
- revise for longer than 2 hours in one sitting
- miss school lessons in order to work alone at home
- try to learn a whole ring-binder's worth of work
- rely on a study guide instead of the text

There are no short-cuts to effective exam revision; the only one way to know a text well, and to know your way around it in an exam, is to have done the necessary studying. If you use the following method, in six easy stages, for both open- and closed-book revision, you will not only revisit and reassess all your previous work on the text in a manageable way but will be able to distil, organise and retain your knowledge. Don't try to do it all in one go: take regular breaks for refreshment and a change of scene.

(1) Between a month and a fortnight before the exam, depending on your schedule (a simple list of stages with dates displayed in your room, not a work of art!), you will need to reread the text, this time taking stock of all the underlinings and marginal annotations as well. As you read, collect onto sheets of A4 the essential ideas and quotations as you come across them. The acts of selecting key material and recording it as notes are natural ways of stimulating thought and aiding memory.

(2) Reread the highlighted areas and marginal annotations in your critical extracts and background handouts, and add anything useful from them to your list of notes and quotations. Then reread your previous essays and the teacher's comments. As you look back through essays written earlier in the course, you should have the pleasant sensation of realising that you can now write much better on the text than you could then. You will also discover that much of your huge file of notes is redundant or repeated, and that you have changed your mind about some beliefs, so that the distillation process is not too daunting. Selecting what is important is the way to crystallise your knowledge and understanding.

(3) During the run-up to the exam you need to do lots of practice essay plans to help you identify any gaps in your knowledge and give you practice in planning in 5–8 minutes. Past paper titles for you to plan are provided in this guide, some of which can be done as full timed essays — and marked strictly according to exam criteria — which will show whether length and timing are problematic for you. If you have not seen a copy of a real exam paper before you take your first module, ask to see a past paper so that you are familiar with the layout and rubric.

(4) About a week before the exam, reduce your two or three sides of A4 notes to a double-sided postcard of very small, dense writing. Collect a group of keywords by once again selecting and condensing, and use abbreviations for quotations (first and last word), and character and place names (initials). (For the comparison unit your postcard will need to refer to key points, themes and quotations in both texts relevant to the specific theme or genre topic.) The act of choosing and writing out the short quotations will help you to focus on the essential issues, and to recall them quickly in the exam. Make sure that your selection covers the main themes and includes examples of symbolism, style, comments on character, examples of irony, point of view or other significant aspects of the text. Previous class discussion and essay writing will have indicated which quotations are useful for almost any title; pick those which can serve more than one purpose, for instance those that reveal character and theme, and are also an example of language. In this way a minimum number of quotations can have maximum application.

(5) You now have in a compact, accessible form all the material for any possible essay title. There are only half a dozen themes relevant to a literary text so if you have covered these, you should not meet with any nasty surprises when you read the exam questions. You don't need to refer to your file of paperwork again, or even to the text. For the few days before the exam, you can read through your handy postcard whenever and wherever you get the opportunity. Each time you read it, which will only take a few minutes, you are reminding yourself of all the information you will be able to recall in the exam to adapt to the general title or to support an analysis of particular passages.

(6) A fresh, active mind works wonders, and information needs time to settle, so don't try to cram just before the exam. Relax the night before and get a good night's sleep. In this way you will be able to enter the exam room with all the confidence of a well-prepared candidate.

Writing examination essays

Essay content

One of the key skills you are being asked to demonstrate at A-level is the ability to select and tailor your knowledge of the text and its background to the question set in the exam paper. In order to reach the highest levels, you need to avoid 'pre-packaged' essays, which lack focus, relevance and coherence, and simply contain everything you know about the text. Be ruthless in rejecting irrelevant material, after considering whether it can be made relevant by a change of emphasis. Aim to cover the whole question, not just part of it; your response needs to demonstrate breadth and depth, covering the full range of text elements: character, event, theme and language. Only half a dozen approaches are possible for any set text, though they may be phrased in a variety of ways, and they are likely to refer to the key themes of the text. Preparation of the text therefore involves extensive discussion and practice at manipulating these core themes so that there should be no surprises in the exam. An apparently new angle is more likely to be something familiar presented in an unfamiliar way and you should not panic or reject the choice of question because you think you know nothing about it.

Exam titles are open-ended in the sense that there is not an obvious right answer, and you would therefore be unwise to give a dismissive, extreme or entirely one-sided response. The question would not have been set if the answer were not debatable. An ability and willingness to see both sides is an Assessment Objective and shows independence of judgement as a reader. Don't be afraid to explore the issues and don't try to tie the text into one neat interpretation. If there is ambiguity, it is likely to be deliberate on the part of the author and must be discussed; literary texts are complex and often paradoxical, and it would be a misreading of them to suggest that there is only one possible interpretation. You are not expected, however, to argue equally strongly or extensively for both sides of an argument, since personal opinion is an important factor. It is advisable to deal with the alternative view at the beginning of your response, and then construct your own view as the main part of the essay. This makes it less likely that you will appear to cancel out your own line of argument.

Choosing the right question

The first skill you must show when presented with the exam paper is the ability to choose the better, for you, of the two questions on your text where there is a choice. This is not to say that you should always go for the same type of essay (whole-text or poem-based), and if the question is not one that you feel happy with for any reason, you should seriously consider the other, even if it is not the type you normally prefer. It is unlikely but possible that a question contains a word you are not sure you know the meaning of, in which case it would be safer to choose the other one.

Don't be tempted to choose a question because of its similarity to one you have already done. Freshness and thinking on the spot usually produce a better product than attempted recall of a previous essay, which may have received only a mediocre mark in the first place. The exam question is unlikely to have exactly the same focus and your response may seem 'off centre' as a result, as well as stale and perfunctory in expression. Essay questions fall into the following categories: close section analysis and relation to whole text; characterisation; setting and atmosphere; structure and effectiveness; genre; language and style; themes and issues. Remember, however, that themes are relevant to all essays and that analysis, not just description, is always required.

Once you have decided which exam question to attempt, follow the procedure below for whole-text and passage-based, open- and closed-book essays.

(1) Underline all the key words in the question and note how many parts the question has.

(2) Plan your answer, using aspects of the key words and parts of the question as sub-headings, in addition to themes. Aim for 10–12 ideas. Check that the Assessment Objectives are covered.

(3) Support your argument by selecting the best examples of characters, events, imagery and quotations to prove your points. Remove ideas for which you can find no evidence.

(4) Structure your answer by grouping and numbering your points in a logical progression. Identify the best general point to keep for the conclusion.

(5) Introduce your essay with a short paragraph setting the context and defining the key words in the question as broadly, but relevantly, as possible.

(6) Write the rest of the essay, following your structured plan but adding extra material if it occurs to you. Paragraph your writing and consider expression, especially sentence structure and vocabulary choices, as you write. Signal changes in the direction of your argument with paragraph openers such as 'Furthermore' and 'However'. Use plenty of short, integrated quotations and use the words of the text rather than your own where possible. Use technical terms appropriately, and write concisely and precisely, avoiding vagueness and ambiguity.

(7) Your conclusion should sound conclusive and make it clear that you have answered the question. It should be an overview of the question and the text, not a repetition or a summary of points already made.

(8) Cross out your plan with a neat, diagonal line.

(9) Check your essay for content, style, clarity and accuracy. With neat crossings-out, correct errors of fact, spelling, grammar and punctuation. Improve expression if possible, and remove any repetition and irrelevance. Add clarification and missing evidence, if necessary, using omission marks or asterisks. Even at this stage, good new material can be added.

There is no such thing as a perfect or model essay; flawed essays can gain full marks. There is always something more which could have been said, and examiners realise that students have limitations when writing under pressure in timed conditions. You are not penalised for what you didn't say in comparison to some idealised concept of the answer, but rewarded for the knowledge and understanding you have shown. It is not as difficult as you may think to do well, provided that you are familiar with the text and have sufficient essay-writing experience. If you follow the above process and **underline, plan, support, structure, write** and **check,** you can't go far wrong.

Text Guidance

Contexts

Assessment Objective 5 requires the candidate to 'evaluate the significance of cultural, historical and other contextual influences on literary texts'. There are a number of contexts in which Larkin's *High Windows* can be viewed.

Biography

The poet, novelist and jazz critic Philip Arthur Larkin was born in Coventry on 9 August 1922. He was the only son and the younger child of Sidney and Eva Larkin. Sidney Larkin, a known Nazi sympathiser and admirer of Adolf Hitler, held the post of City Treasurer of Coventry from 1922 to 1944. As a boy Philip was taken on holiday to Germany, which was by then firmly in the political grip of Nazism. He was taught by his father to admire the achievements of the German nation and, even as an adult, never truly escaped this influence. In 1941, in the face of the Nazi advance, when he was a student at Oxford and feared being called up to fight, Larkin would still not totally distance himself from and denounce Hitler. He observed in a letter to Jim Sutton:

> I expect Pop will be on the lookout for a secondhand copy of Norman Baynes's edition of Hitler's speeches. I looked into them and felt the familiar sinking of heart when I saw how *right* and yet how *wrong* everything had been. The disentanglement of this epoch will be a beautiful job for someone.

The influence of the father on the son is evident in terms of Larkin's character as well as his political views. Sidney Larkin was a highly intelligent but often intolerant man. He possessed a fine library and encouraged his son's bookish tendencies. The odd conditions of life in the Larkin household, where Sidney Larkin's narrow and misogynistic outlook was offset by an unexpected liberality on the subjects of reading and jazz music, no doubt contributed to the many contradictions that emerge in Larkin's subsequent life and writings. He was later to refer to his childhood as 'dull, pot-bound and slightly mad'. In fact, childhood and children remained anathemas to Larkin for the rest of his life. In 'The Savage Seventh', which appears in *Required Writings*, he observes:

> Until I began to meet grown-ups on more or less equal terms I fancied myself a kind of Ishmael. The realisation that it was not people I disliked but children was for me one of those celebrated moments of revelation.

From 1930 to 1940 Larkin attended the King Henry VIII School in Coventry, a boys' grammar school. He was a notoriously quiet and generally unremarkable student in his teachers' eyes, and his copious private writing (he had worked on four novels before he was 18) was largely unknown, except to a few close friends. As he went through the school, however, he began to make contributions to *The Coventrian*, the school magazine, which he coedited from 1939 to 1940.

Oxford years

On leaving school Larkin went up to St John's College, Oxford, again an all-male environment, where he met and developed close friendships with Kingsley Amis and Bruce Montgomery. These connections led to his involvement with what came to be known as the Movement, a group of young English writers, including Larkin, Amis, Donald Davie and Thom Gunn, that rejected the prevailing neo-Romantic trends in the English literary scene (see pp. 18–20). Owing to his poor eyesight, which meant he failed his army medical examination, Larkin was exempted from national service and was therefore able to complete his studies without interruption, gaining a first class honours degree in English. Larkin's educational background no doubt set him apart from many of his Oxford contemporaries, who would have attended public school, and created in him a sense of not belonging to any particular social group.

The love of jazz music Larkin had developed in Coventry grew into a passion in Oxford, and one that he shared with his circle of friends. In his writing during this period he was influenced strongly by W. H. Auden, D. H. Lawrence and W. B. Yeats. The influence of Thomas Hardy, an author Larkin particularly admired, is also evident in his ability to make the commonplace and often dreary elements of day-to-day existence the stuff of tough and uncompromising observation. Larkin's first nationally published poem, 'Ultimatum', appeared in *The Listener* on 28 November 1940.

Librarianship and writing

After graduation, Larkin returned to the family home, which was now in Warwick. He continued to write, spending much time on what was to be his first published novel, *Jill*. He attempted to gain employment in the civil service on two occasions, but failed both times, and eventually took a job as a librarian at Wellington in Shropshire, in November 1943. Full-time employment and part-time study to gain his qualifications as a librarian placed great demands on Larkin's time, but he continued to write and publish. He contributed a selection of early verse to the anthology *Poetry from Oxford in Wartime*, which appeared in 1945, and his first solo collection, *The North Ship*, was published in the same year. These were followed in 1946 by the publication of *Jill*. None of these works received a great deal of public or critical notice. *A Girl in Winter*, however, Larkin's second novel, which was completed in 1945 and published in 1947, attracted some acclaim.

In September 1946 Larkin took a post as assistant librarian at University College, Leicester. He continued his professional studies, becoming a member of the Library Association in 1949. During this period he completed a new collection of poems, entitled *In the Grip of Light*. This, however, was rejected. He moved jobs again in 1950, this time to Belfast, where he was sub-librarian at Queen's University, and began to write again. A small collection, *XX Poems*, was printed privately in 1951. Further poems appeared in pamphlets and a range of other publications, and were eventually gathered into a new collection, *The Less Deceived*, which was published in 1955. It was in this year that Larkin was appointed as librarian in the Brynmor Jones Library at the University of Hull (a post he held until 1985, the year of his death), overseeing the development of the library from a small collection in a ramshackle series of huts to a purpose-built facility with a staff and stock over six times larger than when he started the job.

The Whitsun Weddings, a collection of poems that won wide acclaim, appeared in 1964. This was followed in 1965 by recognition of Larkin's national (and international) standing as a poet in the award of the Queen's Gold Medal for Poetry. His continuing interest in jazz became more concrete at this time; from 1961 to 1971 he was the author of a series of monthly jazz record reviews for the *Daily Telegraph*. A collection of these was published by Faber and Faber as *All What Jazz: a Record Diary (1961–68)* in 1970 (a revised edition appeared in 1985). In 1973 Larkin edited the *Oxford Book of Twentieth Century Verse*. Then, in 1974, came the last of his own volumes of poetry, *High Windows*. By this time his composition of poetry had all but stopped; his last published poem, 'Aubade', appeared in the *Times Literary Supplement* in 1977.

Although there was no more poetry, other books did follow. *Required Writing: Miscellaneous Pieces 1955–82*, a collection of reviews and essays edited by Larkin's friend and literary executor Anthony Thwaite, came out in 1983. *Collected Poems 1938–83* was published after Larkin's death, in 1988. His correspondence appeared posthumously in 1992 as *Selected Letters of Philip Larkin, 1940–85*, and a volume of prose entitled *Further Requirements* was published in 2001, both again edited by Thwaite. Other recent additions to the canon of Larkin's work are *Larkin's Jazz: Essays and Reviews 1940–84*, a further collection of his jazz writings, and *Trouble at Willow Gables and Other Fictions* (edited by James Booth), a set of scurrilous tales that shed light on the author's sexuality.

Public honours and private life

Towards the end of his life, Larkin received a series of awards and honours, including the CBE in 1975. He was the chair of the Booker Prize committee in 1977, and in 1980 became an honorary fellow of the Library Association. In 1982 he was made a professor by the University of Hull, and in 1984 he was created a doctor of letters by the University of Oxford. On the death of his friend Sir John

Betjeman he was offered the position of poet laureate, but declined, as he was no longer composing poetry. Ted Hughes accepted it instead. Shortly before he died he was awarded the Order of the Companion of Honour.

Profoundly influenced by his parents' unhappy marriage, Larkin remained unmarried and childless all his life. It is clear, however, that he was by no means sexually inactive, unlike the personas in a number of his poems (and especially the famous 'Annus Mirabilis' from *High Windows*). He was involved in long-term relationships with three women, the most significant of which was with Monica Jones, a professor of English, with whom he lived. His views on the states of marriage and singleness, and of children, form major **themes** within his literary oeuvre.

Like his father before him (a coincidence of which he was almost fatalistically aware), Larkin died of cancer of the oesophagus at the age of 63. The date of his death was 2 December 1985. He is buried in Cottingham Cemetery in Hull, and his minimalist epitaph reads: 'Philip Larkin 1922–1985 Writer'.

Key dates

1922	Born 9 August, second child and only son of Sidney and Eva Larkin.
1930	Attends King Henry VIII School, Coventry.
1933	Adolf Hitler and his Nazi Party seize power in Germany.
1939	Second World War begins following Hitler's invasion of Poland.
	Coedits *The Coventrian*, his school magazine.
1940	Goes up to Oxford, where he reads for a degree in English. There he meets Kinglsley Amis and Bruce Montgomery.
	'Ultimatum', his first nationally published poem, appears in *The Listener*.
1943	Graduates with a first class honours degree in English. He is allowed to complete his degree and avoid military service because of his poor eyesight.
	In November becomes a librarian at Wellington, Shropshire.
	Meets Ruth Bowman, his first love.
1944	D-Day landings of Allied troops on the Normandy coast signal the beginning of the end of the Second World War.
1945	Contributes to *Poetry from Oxford in Wartime* and publishes *The North Ship*, his first collection of poetry.
	Second World War ends. In its wake, 50 states from around the world create the United Nations.
1946	Publishes *Jill*, his first novel.
	Becomes assistant librarian at University College, Leicester, where he meets Monica Jones.
1947	Publishes *A Girl in Winter*, his last completed novel.
1950	Becomes sub-librarian at Queen's University, Belfast.
1951	Privately publishes *XX Poems*.

1955	Publishes *The Less Deceived*.
	Is appointed librarian at the Brynmor Jones Library, University of Hull.
	Meets Maeve Brennan, later to become his third lover.
1957	The European Economic Community is formed in Rome.
1964	Publishes *The Whitsun Weddings*.
1965	Is awarded the Queen's Gold Medal for Poetry.
1969	Withdrawal of British troops from East Suez.
1970	Publishes *All What Jazz: A Record Diary*.
1973	Edits the *Oxford Book of Twentieth Century Verse*.
1974	Publishes *High Windows*.
1975	Is awarded the CBE.
1977	'Aubade', his last published poem, appears in the *Times Literary Supplement*.
	Chairs the Booker Prize committee.
	Silver Jubilee of Queen Elizabeth II.
1979	Margaret Thatcher and her Conservative government come to power.
1983	Publishes *Required Writings: Miscellaneous Pieces 1955–82*.
1985	Dies 2 December of cancer of the oesophagus, aged 63.

Women and marriage

Larkin and women

Poems like 'High Windows' and 'Annus Mirabilis' present the view of an inexperienced man who has missed the boat in terms of sex and the sexual liberation that began in the magical year of 1963. In reality, what these poems indicate is that public perceptions of sex, and the emotions of secrecy and guilt that formerly surrounded it, changed with the social revolutions of the 1960s. Larkin himself was certainly not sexually inexperienced. In 1945 he had sexual relations with Ruth Bowman, his first love and lover, and as the years progressed he was involved in long-term relationships with both Monica Jones (his lover over many years) and Maeve Brennan (who eventually became his lover in spite of her strong religious views). He also had an affair with Betty Mackereth, who worked in the library at the University of Hull.

This sexual activity would have come as a great surprise to Philip Brown, one of Larkin's contemporaries at Oxford and his roommate, who observed:

> Philip's sexuality was so obscured by his manner of approach and his general diffidence that frankly I would be surprised to hear that he had ever had sex with anyone.

Larkin was clearly good at hiding his true sexual nature — at the very time when he was sharing rooms with Brown, he was writing a series of thinly veiled sexual fantasies and two novels set in an imaginary girls' school, published posthumously as *Trouble at Willow Gables and Other Fictions* (2002). Such voyeuristic and prurient tendencies emerge throughout his writings: an element of sexual fantasy lies at the heart of *Jill*, his first published novel; in 'High Windows' the persona imagines the sexual relationship of a couple he sees walking by; the poem 'Sunny Prestatyn', from *The Whitsun Weddings*, focuses upon the violent and sexually explicit defacing of a poster of a girl in a swimsuit; in 'Wild Oats', from the same collection, the writer is obsessed with the 'bosomy English rose'. This fascination with sex is reflected in Larkin's predilection for collecting pornography. By the end of his life he had amassed a vast quantity of increasingly explicit material, the discovery of which came as a profound shock to Maeve Brennan.

In the light of this it is not surprising to learn that Larkin held some shockingly unenlightened views on the subject of sex and women, often appearing offensive to the reader. His diaries contain a large number of obscene and sometimes misogynistic observations, a selection of which will suffice to make the point:

> The whole business of sex annoys me. As far as I can see, all women are stupid beings.

> Sex is too good to share with anyone else.

> Re sexual intercourse: always disappointing and often repulsive, like asking someone else to blow your own nose for you.

Many of these views, pithily expressed and firmly held, form the basis for Larkin's writings about sex and women. Indeed, sex and writing were closely linked in Larkin's mind, as this extract from a letter written to Jim Sutton on 28 December 1942 makes clear:

> ...writing ha[s] got something to do with sex. I don't know what and I don't particularly want to know. It's not surprising because obviously two creative voices would be in alliance. But the vision has a sexual quality lacking in other emotions such as pity... Ovid, for instance, could never write unless he was in love. Many other poets have been or are the same. I should think poetry and sex are very closely connected.

Larkin's views on sex and women are disconcertingly contradictory. He was capable of the greatest cruelty and heartlessness, a trait perhaps most clearly displayed in his deeply ambivalent relationship with Monica Jones. But her testimony shows that he could be a warm and humorous companion. Although at times duplicitous and deceitful, he was also profoundly loyal. A fear of commitment went alongside an inability to be without a relationship or companionship of some kind. All of these features are reflected in his writings.

Larkin and marriage

Throughout his life Larkin was deeply affected by his parents and their marriage. His father and his mother had extremely different personalities. Both in their own ways had a great influence on him, as he was quick to recognise. In a letter to Jim Sutton of 2 January 1943 he puts it like this:

> I contain both [my mother and my father], and that…is the cause of my inertia, for in me they are incessantly opposed. It intrigues me to know that a thirty year struggle is being continued in me and in my sister too.

The impact of this struggle is famously summed up in Larkin's poem 'This Be The Verse', in which he bluntly observes: 'They fuck you up, your mum and dad./They may not mean to, but they do.' Marriage, parenthood and the relationship between parents and their children form a recurrent theme in Larkin's work. In *The Whitsun Weddings*, poems such as 'Afternoons', 'Take One Home for the Kiddies', 'Self's the Man', 'Talking in Bed', 'The Whitsun Weddings' and 'Dockery and Son' explore his complex feelings on this subject. The almost complete absence of children from *High Windows* could be seen as demonstrating the extent to which Larkin alienated himself from thoughts about them. The fact that his determination never to marry or reproduce was a direct consequence of what he witnessed of his parents' marriage is stated unequivocally in this note from his pocket diary:

> At 1.45 p.m. let me remember that the only married state I know (i.e. that of my parents) is bloody hell. Never must it be forgotten.

It is certain that Larkin never did forget. To the end of his days he fiercely resisted the pressure to marry. Speaking of Larkin's view of marriage, Andrew Motion considers the poem 'Marriages' (from *Collected Poems*), in which Larkin mocks partnerships created by 'old need' and 'scarecrows of chivalry'. Admitting that 'rancour' and self-hatred may seem ignoble reasons for demanding solitude, he also says they are justifiable if they manage to hold marriage at bay (*Philip Larkin: A Writer's Life*, p. 210).

The nearest Larkin was able to come to the marriage commitment, in spite of his tormenting guilt about the way in which he was treating and using women, was to live with Monica Jones for a brief period at the very end of his life, after she had suffered a debilitating illness.

Jazz

Alan Plater, in the foreword to *Larkin's Jazz: Essays and Reviews 1940–84*, dubs Philip Larkin 'the ultimate jazz freak, alone in his room, tapping his feet and snapping his fingers to the music he loves'. Although for many readers of Larkin's poetry such an image may be difficult to conjure up, the connection between the poet of *High Windows* and jazz was long and profound. From early in life Larkin was a confirmed lover of jazz. While he was growing up in Coventry in the 1930s he became acquainted with radio broadcasts of American jazz and blues, and he frequently attended live performances (getting to know a number of the performers) at the local Hippodrome. He even managed to persuade his parents to buy him a drum kit and a set of tuition records, so keen was he to immerse himself in the world of jazz. Later in life he was to observe:

> I was in essence hooked on jazz even before I heard any…what got me was the rhythm.

The extent of the influence of jazz on Larkin emerges in the interview 'Poet on the 8.15' (*Guardian*, 20 May 1965), in which he states: 'I can live a week without poetry but not a day without jazz.' The music of 'trad' jazz and blues artists was arguably his greatest love, and an interest he shared with his fellow members of the Movement (see pp. 18–20), and with Kingsley Amis in particular. It was Larkin's passion, but not an uncritical passion. When discussing later and modernist jazz, forms which he found increasingly distasteful, he was often scathing. His comments on the playing of Miles Davis, the trumpeter, serve to illustrate this:

> …he had several manners: the dead muzzled slow stuff, the sour yelping fast stuff, and the sonorous theatrical arranged stuff, and I disliked them all.

Perhaps this dislike emerged from Larkin's growing sense that jazz was becoming serious, specialist and more overtly 'composed', and that it lacked the easy accessibility of the music he came to love as a young man. (In 'Lives of the Poets' (*Guardian*, 24 November 1961), Larkin regrets the extent to which the arts can become stagnant and lifeless, 'generally accepted and subsidised with unenthusiastic reverence'.) It was the life and passion, the energy and the emotion of jazz that Larkin wished to preserve.

Despite his eminence as a jazz critic and writer, Larkin always (probably disingenuously) claimed the status of an amateur in the field of music. Describing his connection with jazz, he writes:

> I became a jazz addict at the age of twelve or thirteen…and although far from an expert, have never ceased to be an enthusiast.

In a letter to Steve Race, the music critic and broadcaster, and a confirmed lover of modern jazz, he observes:

> I am not a music lover in any real sense of the word; it is only jazz that won my allegiance.

What perhaps lies behind these statements, apart from the self-effacing intentions of a naturally withdrawn and private man, is the recognition that jazz, while a passion, was never for Larkin an academic exercise. *Torchlight 69* (23 October 1962) recounts a talk given by the poet to a group of students at the University of Hull, where he worked as a librarian, in which he offered the view that:

> ...jazz is to be appreciated not as a musical exercise in technique, but as an emotional experience, one that can exhilarate or sadden.

To borrow Paul Oliver's words, it was the ability of jazz and blues (an apt label in the context of Larkin's famously bleak worldview) 'to meet the present world on its own terms' that Larkin so loved.

What Larkin sought in jazz, then, was emotional experience, not academic and intellectual satisfaction. That is not to say, however, that his responses to jazz were lacking in academic and intellectual depth. Whether he realised it or not, he was both learned and sophisticated in his responses to the music he heard. Primarily, though, he revelled in the rhythms and the passions (maybe even the poetry) excited by jazz. Like poetry, jazz was nothing for Larkin if it could not communicate. Writing to Race in 1968, he put forward the following artistic manifesto, which relates to both jazz and poetry:

> What I don't believe about art is that it should require some special knowledge or special training on the part of its consumers. Art is enjoyment first on the part of the writer, painter or musician, and then, by communication, on the part of the reader and looker and listener.

This principle of pleasure provides a fruitful approach both to Larkin's love of jazz music and to his poetry. It is clear that in Larkin's mind the links between the two forms were deep. Writing of Whitney Balliett, jazz columnist for the *New Yorker*, he observes: 'Balliett...brings jazz journalism to the verge of poetry' (*All What Jazz: A Record Diary 1961–71*, p. 212). This is, of course, also true of Larkin's own jazz journalism. Of equal interest to the student of Larkin's poems, however, is the extent to which he brings poetry to the verge of jazz. Poems such as 'For Sidney Bechet' and 'Reference Back', both from *The Whitsun Weddings*, illustrate the ease with which jazz and poetry intermingle and engage with one another in Larkin's imagination.

The Movement

'The Movement' was a term first employed in 1954 by the literary editor of the *Spectator*, J. D. Scott. He used it to describe a group of English writers (writers from Wales and Scotland are generally excluded), the best known of which are Philip

Larkin, Kingsley Amis, Donald Davie, D. J. Enright, John Wain, Elizabeth Jennings and Robert Conquest. The anti-Romantic, witty, sardonic and rational preoccupations of the writers in the Movement are reflected in the three major anthologies they produced during the 1950s and 1960s. The first of these, *Poets of the 1950s*, was published in 1955 in Japan and edited by D. J. Enright. The second, and probably the more famous, is *New Lines*, which appeared in 1956, edited by Robert Conquest. A second *New Lines* came out in 1963, drawing in the work of new poets, such as Anthony Thwaite, Ted Hughes, Vernon Scannell and George MacBeth, though by this time the Movement's heyday as a fashionable artistic force had passed.

The Movement was a looser gathering of writers and a less conscious expression of strongly held views about art than the movements of the early twentieth century, such as imagism, surrealism, Fauvism and futurism. It was more a reflection of negative perceptions of what literature had become. This is perhaps best summed up in the words of Conquest's polemical foreword to *New Lines*, where he describes the connections between the poets as 'little more than a negative determination to avoid bad principles'. The anthology particularly targeted the poets of the 1940s, such as Dylan Thomas and George Barker, though never mentioning them by name. The obscure and overly **metaphorical** nature of their verse was the greatest dislike of the Movement authors, and Conquest promotes the cause of 'rational structure and comprehensible language', both of which are readily identified in the works of Philip Larkin, who is nothing if not clear-spoken.

Main works

The main works of the Movement authors other than Larkin are given in the table below. This list is not comprehensive, nor does it include all the authors associated with the Movement, but reading a selection from it will offer an insight into its literary concerns during the 1950s and early 1960s. Most of these authors continued to write well into the 1980s and some into the 1990s. Blake Morrison's book, *The Movement: English Poetry and Fiction of the 1950s* (1980), is an illuminating account of these writers and their work.

Kingsley Amis	
Poetry	*Bright November* (1947), *A Frame of Mind* (1953)
Novels	Thirty in all, starting with *Lucky Jim* (1954), *That Uncertain Feeling* (1955) *I Like It Here* (1958) and *Take a Girl Like You* (1960)
John Braine	
Novels	*Room at the Top* (1957), *Life at the Top* (1962)
Robert Conquest	
Poetry	*Poems* (1955), *Between Mars and Venus* (1962), *Arias from a Love Opera* (1969)

Donald Davie	
Poetry	*Brides of Reason* (1955), *A Winter Talent* (1957)
Criticism	*Purity of Diction in English Verse* (1952)
D. J. Enright	
Poetry	*The Laughing Hyena and Other Poems* (1953), *Bread Rather Than Blossoms* (1956)
Novel	*Insufficient Poppy* (1960)
Criticism	*Man is an Onion: Reviews and Essays* (1972)
Ted Hughes	
Poetry	*The Hawk in the Rain* (1957), *Lupercal* (1960)
Prose and verse	*Wodwo* (1967)
Elizabeth Jennings	
Poetry	*Poems* (1953), *A Way of Looking* (1955), *A Sense of the World* (1958)
George MacBeth	
Poetry	*A Form of Words* (1954), *The Colour of Blood* (1967)
Vernon Scannell	
Poetry	*Graves and Resurrections* (1948), *The Masks of Love* (1960) *Sense of Danger* (1962)
Anthony Thwaite	
Poetry	*Home Truths* (1957), *The Stones of Emptiness: Poems 1963–66* (1967)
John Wain	
Poetry	*Poems 1949–79* (1980)
Novels	*Hurry on Down* (1953), *The Contenders* (1958), *A Travelling Woman* (1959)

The 1960s

The 1960s was a significant decade in British history. The period of austerity which began during the Second World War did not end until the early 1950s. Rationing of food and other items continued until 1954, by which time Larkin had already published two novels, *Jill* and *A Girl in Winter*, and two collections of poetry, *The North Ship* and *XX Poems*. During the late 1950s a number of changes occurred: pop music began to emerge (there is an **allusion** to this in 'Annus Mirabilis', where Larkin identifies the year 1963 by 'the end of the *Chatterley* ban/And the Beatles' first LP'); film became an important influence on young people; televisions and telephones were installed in many British homes. Together, these led to the revolution of mass media and mass communications.

Post-colonial Britain

Britain was a major imperial power until the Second World War: the British Empire was the largest in the world and spanned the globe. After the war it became clear that the era of empire was over, and the granting of independence to India, Pakistan and Ceylon as early as 1947 was a precursor to the process of wholesale decolonisation which began in the late 1950s (see 'Naturally the Foundation will

Bear Your Expenses' in *The Whitsun Weddings*). This led to two major changes in British society. The first was the mass immigration of non-European people from former colonies, which in time turned Britain into a multiracial society. This was controversial; racism became an issue, and was whipped up by right-wing nationalist politicians, perhaps most famously Enoch Powell. The second change was more subtle: from being a major world power, Britain slowly became a small country in Europe, and many people had difficulty in coming to terms with Britain's loss of importance and influence on the world stage. These changes and Britain's apparent decline are significant in *High Windows* and are dealt with in 'Going, Going', in which the country is visualised as gradually degenerating and metaphorically disappearing.

Politics and culture

Britain has been a democracy since the nineteenth century, but a combination of factors led to the right-wing Conservative Party dominating British politics for much of the twentieth century. The left-wing Labour party came to power in 1964, after 13 years of Conservative rule, and the new government coincided with a period of renewed intellectual and cultural life in the country. It was the era of the Beatles, the most successful pop group ever, of 'Swinging Britain', with its outrageous fashion and personal liberation. The widespread introduction of the contraceptive pill meant that women could have sex without fear of becoming pregnant, and by the end of the 1960s the 'sexual revolution' had swept away centuries of taboos. Larkin approaches these issues explicitly in 'Annus Mirabilis', in which he states that 'Sexual intercourse began/In nineteen sixty three', and in 'High Windows', where he looks on enviously at the overt sexual freedom of a young couple, a contrast to his own 'hidden' sex life. 'Free love' became popular and male homosexuality became legal for the first time. The 'hippy' movement of the late 1960s seemed to promise an alternative lifestyle that was unconventional, anti-materialist and free-thinking. All these changes broke the stranglehold of conventional morality and class **stereotyping** that for some had made life in the 1950s and early 1960s stifling. In Larkin's work, however, conservative attitudes continue to hold sway, as if he is a repository of older, outmoded values. This generates a sense of the poet as an outsider, observing a world to which he does not really seem to belong. Political views emerge in 'Homage to a Government', in which Larkin employs an openly and **ironically** outspoken voice, though whether the views expressed are his own is unclear.

Social change

The many social changes of the 1960s particularly affected young people and women. This was the era of pop-art, mini-skirts, beat music, long hair and hallucinogenic

drugs. Young people went to pop festivals and love-ins, and joined the peace movement (which grew out of the Campaign for Nuclear Disarmament).

The feminist movement began to challenge all the limitations placed upon women, and there was a feeling among intelligent young women that everything was possible. Grammar schools offered a route to university for lower-middle-class women who would previously never have considered going, such as Margaret Thatcher (a woman Larkin greatly admired and who subsequently became prime minister). The development of labour-saving domestic appliances, such as washing machines, reduced the burden of domestic tasks. Women increasingly challenged the traditional view that their place was in the home and chose to make careers for themselves.

For Philip Larkin's generation, which had grown up under the deprivations and hardships of the Second World War and the postwar era, the 1960s, with its seemingly limitless freedoms, was a time of ambivalence. While the new freedoms were welcomed by some, they were resented by many and vilified by others. In poems like 'Annus Mirabilis' and 'High Windows' Larkin may celebrate the newfound and overt sexual opportunities that came with increased sexual freedom for women, but in poems such as 'A Study of Reading Habits' and 'Sunny Prestatyn' in *The Whitsun Weddings* a more disturbing sense of women as sex objects emerges. The changing face of England and its mores is the subject of a number of poems in *High Windows*, notably 'Going, Going' and 'How Distant'. This theme is particularly evident in Larkin's presentation of the growth of the consumer culture, with its attendant emphasis on advertising. He deals with this issue directly in 'Going, Going' and 'How Distant', where the aggressive marketing of places and consumer products is a central issue.

Language

When studying the work of any author it is essential to focus closely on the characteristics of his or her language and to consider its effects in depth. Some of the significant characteristics of Larkin's language are explored below.

Range

Larkin's poetry is notable for the wide range of language it employs, varying from the highly poetic to the obscene. His combination of different registers in *High Windows* generates a number of effects. Its realistic synthesis of the moving, the obscene, the elevated, the base, and so on, communicates to a variety of audiences and appeals to a number of emotions. However, it also creates an uneasy sense of linguistic dislocation and might even be said to construct a redefinition of what constitutes 'poetic' diction.

The following table illustrates the variety of tones and registers in *High Windows*.

Precise and incisive description	Qualified or tentative phrasing
'a big sky/Drains down the estuary like the bed/Of a gold river' 'Livings I'	'The trees are coming into leaf/Like something almost being said' 'The Trees'
'On tiny decks past fraying cliffs of water' 'How Distant'	'Though white is not my favourite colour.' 'Sympathy in White Major'
'All round it close-ribbed streets rise and fall' 'The Building'	'teaching their children by a sort/Of clowning' 'To the Sea'
'Light spreads darkly downwards from the high/Clusters of lights' 'Friday Night in the Royal Station Hotel'	'The headed paper, made for writing home/(If home existed)' 'Friday Night in Night in the Royal Station Hotel'
'Rather than words comes the thought of high windows:/The sun-comprehending glass' 'High Windows'	'(Which was rather late for me)' 'Annus Mirabilis'
Colloquial, unpoetic language	**Intense, poetic diction and description**
'(Quicker than going to the bogs)' 'Livings III'	'Lozenge of love! Medallion of art!' 'Sad Steps'
'Oh, you know the thing,/That crummy textbook stuff from Freshman Psych' 'Posterity'	'Creatures, I cherish you!' 'Livings' II
'I just think it will happen, soon.' 'Going, Going'	'Last year is dead, they seem to say,/Begin afresh, afresh, afresh.' 'The Trees'
'Their looks show that they're for it' 'The Old Fools'	'the deep blue air, that shows/Nothing, and is nowhere, and is endless.' 'High Windows'
'girls with hair-dos' 'The Building'	'something they share/That breaks ancestrally each year into/Regenerate union. Let it always be there.' 'Show Saturday'
Coarse and obscene language	**Sharp, dismissive diction**
'When I see a couple of kids/And guess he's fucking her' 'High Windows'	'"I'm stuck with this old fart at least a year"' 'Posterity'
'Jan van Hogspeuw staggers to the door/And pisses at the dark.' 'The Card-Players'	'I wanted them over,/Hurried to burial' 'Forget What Did'
'you keep on pissing yourself' 'The Old Fools'	'Well,/We shall find out.' 'The Old Fools'
'They fuck you up, your mum and dad' 'This Be The Verse'	'Get out as early as you can,/And don't have any kids yourself.' 'This Be The Verse'
'My wife and I have asked a crowd of craps/To come and waste their time and ours' 'Vers de Société'	*'All solitude is selfish'* 'Vers de Société'
'In a pig's arse, friend.' 'Vers de Société'	'"I am all you never had of goods and sex."' 'Money'
	'Births, deaths. For sale. Police court. Motor spares.' 'Livings I'

Hyphenated words

Throughout *High Windows* Larkin uses hyphenated words to create precise meanings through word combination:

- The 'oath-edged talk and pipe-smoke' of the miners in 'The Explosion' creates a sense of routine and camaraderie.
- 'Show Saturday' contains a number of examples, all of which evoke precise **images** of objects and, particularly, people: 'Stiff-legged' wrestlers, 'shining-

leafed cabbages', 'dog-breeding wool-defined women', 'Children all saddle-swank', 'car-tuning curt-haired sons'.

- Images of nature are sharply depicted in combinations such as 'wind-picked sky' ('Sad Steps'), 'moon thinned/To an air-sharpened blade' ('Vers de Société'), 'young-leafed June' and 'high-builded cloud' ('Cut Grass'), 'Tree-muffled squares' ('Homage to a Government'), 'wet century-wide trees' ('The Card-Players').
- The evening of life is poignantly evoked in 'some lonely/Rain-ceased midsummer evening' ('The Old Fools').
- In 'Going, Going' England appears to be disappearing beneath 'greeds/And garbage…too thick-strewn'.
- The contradictions of parenthood and parenting are summed up in the **antithetical** combination of 'soppy-stern' ('This Be The Verse').
- 'High Windows' ends with the warm and visionary image of 'sun-comprehending glass'.

Negative language

Throughout *High Windows* there are numerous words beginning with the prefixes im-, in- and un- or ending with the suffix -less to indicate negativity. The accumulation of these negative forms emphasises the extent to which Larkin's verse entails negative definition: things are frequently described by what they are not rather than what they are. This leaves a sense of inadequacy and unfulfilment, the feeling that there is something lacking. The repeated use of negatives throughout *High Windows* ('no', 'not', 'none', 'never', 'nothing', 'nobody', 'nowhere', 'no one', etc.) also creates a sense of definition through absence. The accretion of such vocabulary contributes to the pervading sense of negativity that underlies Larkin's famously bleak worldview.

The table below categorises these negative forms.

im-	impatience, immobile
in-	incompetent, incurious
un-	unresting, undressed, unsown, unsold, unfurnished, unspoilt, unreal, unseen, undiminished, unaided, unrecompensed, unclosing, uncertain, unlosable, unharmed, unbalance, unbroken
-less	cloudless, flawless, endlessly, endless, shoeless, starlessness

Themes

The key themes of *High Windows* are listed below, with details of poems in which each appears and comments on how it is treated.

Isolation and community

Isolation is at the heart of all Larkin's writing and plays a central role in *High Windows*. Whereas some poems in *The Whitsun Weddings*, such as 'The Importance of Elsewhere' and 'Here', express positive experiences of solitude and remoteness, in *High Windows* isolation is generally presented much more negatively.

Community is also a recurrent element in *High Windows*. Sometimes human company and society are sources of pleasure or comfort, but frequently the proximity of others serves only to increase an individual's sense of isolation.

The table below identifies which poems address isolation, community or both.

Poem	Isolation	Community	Isolation and community
'To the Sea'			✔
'Sympathy in White Major'		✔	
'Livings I'			✔
'Livings II'			✔
'Livings III'			✔
'Forget What Did'	✔		
'High Windows'			✔
'Friday Night in the Royal Station Hotel'			✔
'The Old Fools'			✔
'Going, Going'			✔
'The Card-Players'			✔
'The Building'			✔
'Posterity'			✔
'Dublinesque'		✔	
'Homage to a Government'		✔	
'This Be The Verse'	✔		
'How Distant'		✔	
'Sad Steps'	✔		
'Solar'	✔		
'Annus Mirabilis'			✔
'Vers de Société'			✔
'Show Saturday'		✔	
'Money'		✔	
'The Explosion'			✔

Isolation

Experiences of isolation and loneliness pervade *High Windows*. The hotel in 'Friday Night in the Royal Station Hotel' is deserted in the absence of the weekday businessmen; the **persona** experiences a 'larger loneliness' and realises 'How/Isolated' he is in this place of 'exile'. In 'Livings I' the travelling salesman takes a single room and in the empty square comes to realise the loneliness of his existence and the need for change. The persona in 'High Windows' is conscious of his isolation from the society that surrounds him; the parentheses in 'Annus Mirabilis' express the isolation the persona feels in having missed sexual liberation; 'The Old Fools' find themselves

disconnected from their bodies, their lives and other people; the patients in 'The Building' are isolated from the rest of the world.

But Larkin also represents isolation as desirable. The persona of 'Vers de Société' would prefer to cut himself off, but feels obliged to be part of the social round; the image of the hermit evokes solitude, but the power of choosing to 'be alone freely' is seen as a luxury enjoyed only by the young. 'This Be The Verse' advocates isolation through not having children.

Community

A variety of social and community events are represented in *High Windows*. These include:

- going to hospital ('The Building')
- the seaside holiday ('To the Sea')
- going to a hotel ('Livings I' and 'Friday Night in the Royal Station Hotel')
- eating dinner ('Livings I' and 'Livings III')
- funerals ('Sympathy in White Major', 'Dublinesque' and 'The Explosion')
- the rural show ('Show Saturday')
- a card game ('The Card-Players')
- meeting friends ('Posterity')
- drinks parties and going to church ('Vers de Société')

'To the Sea' and 'The Explosion' represent community as providing a shared experience of pleasure or of mutual support in the face of sadness and bereavement. 'This Be The Verse', 'Friday Night in the Royal Station Hotel', 'The Building' and 'Forget What Did' perhaps show that the absence of meaningful human interaction generates negative perspectives on life. However, 'Money', 'Dublinesque', 'How Distant', 'High Windows', 'Annus Mirabilis' and 'Show Saturday' present community as a repository of social, religious and moral values, some of which are positive (e.g. compassion in bereavement) and some negative (e.g. materialism).

Isolation within a community

Isolation is sometimes most acutely and corrosively experienced in the context of company or community. This idea is explored in a number of poems:

- 'The Explosion' — within the context of collective bereavement, the poem hones in on the image of one dead man carrying a nest of lark's eggs, and this in turn brings into focus the idea of one particular widow's loss and sorrow.
- 'The Old Fools' — the company of other old people who are experiencing the same physical and mental deterioration does not prevent the very elderly from suffering feelings of helplessness and anguished solitude.
- 'The Building' — fear and loneliness in the face of illness and possible death set the patients in the hospital apart from the surrounding world. The presence of

nurses and visitors who are in possession of their health serves only to underline this contrast.

- 'Annus Mirabilis' — the change in sexual mores creates a pronounced sense of social isolation in the persona and alienates him from his own sexual feelings.
- 'Friday Night in the Royal Station Hotel' — the emptiness of the hotel and the persona's sense of isolation in it are emphasised by his consciousness that the guests who were there during the week have now departed.
- 'Vers de Société' — the persona sees social intercourse as pointless, underlining how antisocial he has grown with his increasing years. At the same time, he fears that if he withdraws from such socialising altogether he will be left alone with his feelings of 'failure and remorse'.

Disillusionment and futility

This theme appears throughout much of Larkin's poetry and fiction. In 'Friday Night in the Royal Station Hotel' the guest experiences a dispiriting revelation of emptiness and unfulfilment; in 'Vers de Société' the persona is disillusioned with what he perceives to be a futile round of social engagements. The salesman of 'Livings I' is left 'wondering why/I think it's worth while coming'; the diarist of 'Forget What Did' evidently believes his life is futile, and that continuing to keep a diary would be a waste of time and effort; 'Money' makes clear the worthlessness of money and the illusory nature of the happiness it is believed to bring.

In 'The Old Fools' old age is represented as the helpless culmination of a pointless existence, while 'The Building' makes clear the futility of hoping to avoid illness and eventual death. The persona of 'Going, Going' is disillusioned by the radical and unpleasant changes he sees England undergoing, whereas 'Homage to a Government' explores political disillusionment.

Youth and age

The persona's visit to the seaside in 'To the Sea' makes him conscious of successive generations of holidaymakers, from 'uncertain children' to the 'rigid old'. 'High Windows', 'Annus Mirabilis', 'Going, Going' and 'How Distant' portray the changes in society and its mores through contrasts between the generations. In 'Posterity', the persona's age and old-fashioned style provoke scorn on the part of Balokowsky, who sums his subject up as 'one of those old-type *natural* fouled-up guys'.

Although the annual cycle of decay and new growth of 'The Trees' implies that, unlike people, they do not age, the rings in their trunks record their inexorable progress towards death. 'The Old Fools' and 'Sad Steps' explore the effects of ageing on the body and the mind, and in 'The Building' both young and old are present in the hospital, but the persona emphasises the irrelevance of age in the face of illness and inevitable death. 'This Be The Verse' explores the unwelcome legacies passed on from parents to their children.

Death

Death is a recurrent concern in *High Windows* and throughout Larkin's work. In 'The Old Fools' he refers to death as 'The peak that stays in view wherever we go', indicating a perpetual awareness of death and providing an apt metaphor for his own poetic oeuvre. In Larkin's world, death is an integral part of life, and this does not just mean literal death: deaths of places, ways of life, personality and hope occur too. The table below identifies where different types of death appear.

Poem	Physical death	Death of a place	Death of a way of life
'To the Sea'	✔		
'Sympathy in White Major'	✔		
'The Trees'	✔		
'Livings I'	✔		✔
'Livings II'	✔		
'Livings III'	✔		
'Forget What Did'			✔
'High Windows'			✔
'Friday Night in the Royal Station Hotel'		✔	
'The Old Fools'	✔		✔
'Going, Going'		✔	✔
'The Building'	✔		
'Dublinesque'	✔		
'Homage to a Government'			✔
'This Be The Verse'			
'How Distant'			✔
'Sad Steps'	✔		
'Solar'			
'Annus Mirabilis'			✔
'Vers de Société'			
'Money'			
'Cut Grass'	✔		
'The Explosion'	✔		✔

Physical death

'The Old Fools' paints a bleak and uncompromising portrait of the onset of death, foregrounding the failing bodies and faculties of the very elderly. Death and illness are powerful presences in 'The Building'. Death affects everyone: 'All know they are going to die./Not yet, perhaps not here, but in the end,/And somewhere like this.' Death and bodily decay are seen as inevitable states for all humanity, masked by an illusion of health and well-being: 'conceits/And self-protecting ignorance congeal/To carry life, collapsing only when//Called to these corridors.' The persona emphasises the inescapability of the hospital and the death that many patients will meet there: 'O world,/Your loves, your chances, are beyond the stretch/Of any hand from here!' The unexpected deaths in 'The Explosion' are a similar reminder that humanity merely deludes itself that death is a distant and unlikely event: it is in fact an ever-present reality. The poem also looks half comfortingly and half scathingly at the consolations of religion and conceptions of eternity. More positively, the continuation of life is present in the final image of the unbroken eggs.

The treatment of death in 'Dublinesque' is poignant and bittersweet. The poem evokes the Irish commemoration of death, capturing the dichotomy between the 'great friendliness', the camaraderie and the music of the occasion and the overwhelming personal sadness in the final stanza. 'Sympathy in White Major' offers a semi-affectionate view of death; the deceased is presented as good and likeable, but the value of his existence is at the same time cynically undermined, especially in the final line of the poem.

Larkin represents death as part of the natural cycle in 'Cut Grass', 'The Trees' and 'To the Sea'. In 'The Trees', death forms part of the fruitful annual cycle, without which new life would not be possible. In 'To the Sea', the 'rigid old' are evidently near to death, but are seen as part of the cycle of life, tended by the families who have brought them to the sea, which is like a life source.

Physical death enters 'Livings III' through references to Judas, the disciple whose betrayal of Jesus to the Jewish and Roman authorities led to his crucifixion, and Jack Ketch, the archetypal figure of the executioner. These form a darkly humorous part of the mealtime conversation.

Death of a place

The absence of the weekday clientele of businessmen and salesmen in 'Friday Night in the Royal Station Hotel' leaves the hotel a lifeless and empty place. Details such as the unsold evening paper, the idle porter and the dirty ashtrays are all expressive of inactivity and desolation.

'Going, Going' envisages the death of England as the persona knows it. The humorous tone does not conceal the underlying sadness he feels at the passing of the idyllic and predominantly rural England he loves and wishes to see preserved. **Rhythm** and pace are handled so as to convey unstoppable momentum towards destruction.

Death of a way of life

'High Windows' and 'Annus Mirabilis' deal with social change and the death of an outdated set of mores and conventions. In the latter, this is exemplified by the lifting of the ban on D. H. Lawrence's novel *Lady Chatterley's Lover* and the immense popular success of the Beatles. An old 'innocence' (or perhaps an old hypocrisy) is seen to have died.

In 'Livings I' the old way of earning a living by selling 'dips and feed' is no longer viable. The father's death prompts the son to end the family business and the way of life that goes with it. 'Forget What Did' describes how the dull

regularity of life, as represented by the daily writing of the diary, is terminated, and creates a broader sense that the persona's existence is a living death. The cynical tone of 'Homage to a Government' implies that honour and principle in politics have died.

Death of a personality

In 'Livings I', the salesman, while convinced that it is 'time for a change', is aware of the **pathos** of his decision to end the family business. The poem evokes an acute sense of loss, exemplified in the image of the declining sun in stanza 3. The ending of the business is somehow a betrayal of the father, a killing of his personality and a destruction of his legacy.

When the persona in 'Forget What Did' ceases to write his diary he effectively kills himself. The recognition that his life means nothing is profoundly disconcerting, a 'stun' not only to memory but to his entire sense of identity. Individual existence is represented as worthless except insofar as it is subsumed within the cycles of the natural world.

Time

In *High Windows*, as elsewhere in Larkin's work, markers of time — minutes, hours, days, seasons, years, centuries etc. — represent the ways in which we measure our lives.

In 'Livings III', the phrase 'the bells discuss the hour's gradations' emphasises the dullness of the dinner conversation and the relentless progress of time. 'Vers de Société' questions whether social intercourse is a waste of time; a reference to the limited lifespan remaining to the persona, 'time is shorter now', doubles as an allusion to the way in which perceptions of time change with age. Similar details sharpen the focus on the passage of time or specific times of day in 'Friday Night in the Royal Station Hotel', 'The Building', 'Sad Steps', 'Money', 'Cut Grass' and 'The Explosion'. In 'The Trees' references to 'yearly' and 'last year' emphasise the passage of time and the vision of 'Wet century-wide trees' in 'The Card-Players' is a vivid temporal image. In 'The Building' a nostalgic note is struck by the image of the terraced houses surrounding the hospital as 'a great sigh out of the last century'.

The show in 'Show Saturday' marks the shift of season from 'summer' to 'winter coming'; it also represents an unchanging ritual that helps people forget their ultimate fate, a reminder of which occurs in the lines 'time's rolling smithy-smoke/Shadows much greater gestures'. 'To the Sea' deals with the repetitive cycle of time and the endurance of the British seaside holiday; the opening lines of the poem enact the process of stepping back in time.

'High Windows' traces a shift from concrete time to abstract time, paralleling the poem's movement from the bodily to the spiritual; it begins with 'outdated' and 'forty years back', but concludes with the 'endless', eternal vistas of the skies.

Similarly, 'Solar' offers a metaphysical, quasi-religious perspective on time: 'Our needs hourly/Climb and return like angels./Unclosing like a hand,/You give forever.' 'The Old Fools' explores the impact of time on the elderly and their efforts to relive, recapture or reverse time.

More specific time references occur elsewhere. In 'Livings I' — the date at the end of this part of the poem is offered as a significant marker — the end of a decade and a family tradition. Specific dates are important in 'Annus Mirabilis', in which 1963 becomes a symbolic year of liberation, and 'Homage to a Government', which is ascribed to the year 1969. In 'Posterity', Balokowsky complains that he is 'stuck with this old fart at least a year'; although he begrudges the time it will take to write the biography, his casual writing off of this period demonstrates an unconsciousness of his own mortality, which is one of the luxuries of youth.

Routine and cycles

Many of the examples discussed in relation to time are also relevant to the concepts of routine and cycles in *High Windows*. Time is represented not only as a linear force, but also as a cyclical one, turning continually back upon itself to create endless repeated patterns and an almost fatalistic sense of inevitability.

'To the Sea' looks at the 'annual rite' of the summer holiday, with parents passing the shared experience on to their children. The annual rural show in 'Show Saturday' is represented as a symbol of seasonal cycles, the social round and repeated pleasure. In contrast, the salesman persona in 'Livings I' describes how 'Every third month I book myself in at/The ------ Hotel in ----ton for three days': this mundane cycle is a source of boredom. The poem also deals with breaking generational repetition within the family business. 'Forget What Did' describes the breaking of a meaningless human cycle (writing the diary) but ascribes value to cycles in nature ('Celestial recurrences,/The days the flowers come,/And when the birds go'). Natural cycles also occur in 'Sad Steps' and 'Solar', which adopt the concept of celestial cycles as significant influences upon humanity, and 'The Trees', in which the focus on annual rebirth and the suggestive use of the image of concentric rings suggests cycles and fruitful repetition.

'High Windows' considers the envious view of the young that is taken by each generation of the old and looks at cycles of social change. In 'The Old Fools' the elderly replay the events of their lives in their fading memories; the inevitability of ageing and its repetition in all of us is emphasised at the end ('Well,/We shall find out'). 'This Be The Verse' looks at generational repetition and the negative impact that successive generations of parents have upon their children; the persona advocates breaking the cycle by remaining childless. 'Annus Mirabilis' uses modified repetition in the opening and final stanzas to illustrate the cycle of social change the poem explores.

Imagery

Windows

Windows are the most significant images in the collection. Larkin uses windows to express reflection, detachment and concealment — what is seen and what is not seen. Windows are sources of light, providing contact between the internal and the external, and allowing a point of vantage and a view of other worlds. Examples include the following:

- 'Sad Steps' recounts an epiphany experienced at an upstairs window.
- 'Money' asks the reader to imagine himself or herself 'looking down/From long french windows at a provincial town'. This perspective seems to detach the viewer from reality, allowing a view of potential that cannot be fulfilled.
- In 'The Building' patients look down from high windows at the world of normality that is carrying on without them.
- 'How Distant' leaves the reader with the image of 'random windows conjuring a street', creating an uneasy sense of incompleteness and uncertainty.
- In 'Forget What Did' windows are used in a very different way — not as apertures for insight and observation but as the means of self-protecting concealment: the diarist leaves things too pointless and painful to be remembered 'Missing behind the windows/Of an opaque childhood'.

Religion

There is a significant body of religious imagery in *High Windows*, suggesting a spiritual and reflective sensibility, though not a conventionally devout or pious one. It is interesting that when Larkin uses religious imagery this often has the effect of condemning religion itself.

In 'To the Sea', the annual visit to the seaside is described as 'half an annual pleasure, half a rite', and in 'Show Saturday' competitors display 'blanch leeks like church candles', suggesting that these events have a significance for the partici-pants like that of religious worship for churchgoers. The carved choirs in 'Going, Going' are a symbol of the England and its traditions that are being lost to modernity — a nostalgic view of religion that makes it part of a threatened social fabric.

However, the 'locked church' in 'The Building' perhaps suggests that organised religion is enclosed and exclusive. The patients are there to 'confess that something has gone wrong'; they are 'unseen congregations', as if they are there to praise some deity. In 'Vers de Société' 'No one now/Believes the hermit with his gown and dish/Talking to God (who's gone too)', highlighting Larkin's interest in isolation but also suggesting that society has discarded religion. The poem uses religious language in a different way when it questions whether social routines are simply 'Playing at goodness, like going to church' — churchgoing in this case is a symbol of hypocrisy.

In 'High Windows' the absence of religion is even perceived as liberating: '*That'll be the life;/No God any more, or sweating in the dark//About Hell and that, or having to hide/What you think of the priest.*' Religion appears to be a restrictive and menacing force of social control.

Colour

The table below identifies the colours that feature in the poems in *High Windows* and their impact and connotations.

Colour(s)	Poems(s)	Impact and connotations
blue water, red bathing caps, yellow sand	'To the Sea'	provides sense of brightness and gaiety; helps establish the festive mood of holiday
white	'To the Sea'	the colour of the children's clothes suggests innocence
	'Sympathy in White Major'	carries the sense of being a good sport; also associated with death, so the persona's dislike of the colour white implies reluctance to die
	'Cut Grass'	the 'white hours' suggests heat; the various white flowers and blossoms symbolise beauty and innocence
	'The Building'	the dead are visualised in 'white rows'
green	'The Trees'	sign of new life, but also 'a kind of grief', foreshadowing death
gold	'The Explosion'	preciousness, radiance, a wealth the dead men did not possess when living
	'Livings I'	beauty, wealth
	'Solar'	beauty, heat, wealth
grape-dark, leather-black	'Livings II'	disturbing, violent and threatening colours which mirror the sea
deep blue air	'High Windows'	openness, freedom, peace, the ethereal and eternal
ash hair	'The Old Fools'	greyness, fading, lack of definition, loss of colour and life, cremation
grey	'Going, Going'	'Grey area grants' is a humorous inversion of green area grants; suggests England becoming monochrome, lack of definition, loss of colour and life
	'Show Saturday'	'Grey day' implies inauspicious weather; 'grey-haired' refers to age
	'Dublinesque'	the pewter light suggests greyness and loss of life
red	'The Building'	the red brick implies respectability, solidity, but also perhaps blood
green and white	'How Distant'	colours establish the contrast and distance (both physical and psychological) between land and sea

The sea

In some poems Larkin uses the sea to symbolise endurance. The seaside holiday in 'To the Sea' represents lasting Britishness (Britain has always been a seafaring nation), and provides a refreshing annual routine. In 'Going, Going' the sea is shown to be resilient and enduring even in the face of man's attempts to destroy it: 'Chuck filth in the sea, if you must:/The tides will be clean beyond.' In the lighthouse of 'Livings II' the mussels and limpets are admired for their tenacity and provide strangely comforting company, although the sea itself can be a powerful, threatening and destructive force.

However, sea imagery has different connotations elsewhere. In 'The Building', the hospital is described as a 'clean-sliced cliff', and in 'This Be The Verse', misery 'deepens like a coastal shelf'. Both of these images refer to strata, suggesting the passage of time and the succession of generations.

Money

Money imagery is linked to Larkin's perceptions of a changing and consumerist society:

- In the poem 'Money', unspent money represents wasted opportunities for goods and sex. Money is the measure of life in a consumer society but ultimately 'Won't…buy you more than a shave'. Although it sings like a siren, it proves to be essentially empty and 'intensely sad'.
- In 'Show Saturday' one of the less trustworthy entertainers ('a quack of a man') is associated with venality by 'pound notes round his hat'.
- 'Livings I' is about a travelling salesman and conversation is centred on money issues, revolving around 'Who makes ends meet, who's taking the knock,/Government tariffs, wages, price of stock'.
- In 'Going, Going' greed is represented by the children 'screaming for more' and businessmen gloating over 'Some takeover bid that entails/Five per cent profit (and ten/Per cent more in the estuaries)'.
- The sexual revolution discussed in 'Annus Mirabilis' is described as 'A brilliant breaking of the bank'. This metaphor suggests the difficulty of achieving such freedom, and also makes clear the perceived 'riches' which result.

Clouds

Clouds are often associated with hardship or trouble, but Larkin uses them in a number of ways to convey different meanings. The clouds in 'Show Saturday' are innocuous; although it is a 'Grey day', this does nothing to dampen the spirits of the crowds. Similarly, in the 'unfurnished sky' of 'Solar' and the 'cloudless scene' of 'To the Sea', the absence of clouds betokens freedom from difficulties and hardship — both are strikingly positive poems. In 'Cut Grass' the sky carries a 'high-builded cloud/Moving at summer's pace', reflecting both the laziness of a warm day and the more sinister images of decay earlier in the poem. The wind-rent clouds of 'Sad Steps', which startle the persona (stanza 1) and are disturbingly compared to 'cannon-smoke' in stanza 3, are more ominous. These clouds are a symbol of the inexorable forces of nature, rushing the persona on towards old age.

Fragmentation

Larkin uses images of fragmentation to show death, decay and loss. In 'The Old Fools', we are told: 'At death, you break up: the bits that were you/Start speeding away from each other'. The poem explores how this process of uncreation begins even before death with the fragmentation of bodily function and memory. The fragmentation caused by death is also important in 'The Explosion', 'Dublinesque' and 'Sympathy in White Major', though in these poems it is explored from the perspectives of those left behind. The dissolution of the body that occurs with coming age is examined in 'Sad Steps', where the fractured clouds provide an image of fragmentation.

Elsewhere, the ongoing or imminent loss of traditional aspects of English life represents the fragmentation of the social fabric. This can be seen in 'Show Saturday', 'Going, Going', 'Forget What Did' and 'Livings I'.

Sun, moon and stars

The heavens and the heavenly bodies are repeated motifs in *High Windows*.

- They appear at the end of 'Livings III', where the 'Chaldean constellations/ Sparkle over crowded roofs'. This is a sudden opening of light and hope in the dark night, and an image of freedom after the claustrophobic and lonely domesticity depicted earlier in the poem.
- Stars also appear in 'How Distant', where the 'differently-swung stars' cast a beneficent light.
- In 'Forget What Did' the heavens provide a contrast to the mundane realities of life; 'Celestial recurrences' is one of the subjects the persona considers it worth entering should anyone fill in the empty pages in the future.
- In 'The Card-Players' the 'starlessness' of the skies suggests the absence of light and hope.
- 'Sad Steps' and 'Solar' deal with the major heavenly bodies, the sun and the moon. Both are presented as powerful, living forces looking down on and influencing the lives of humans. Unlike the moon in 'Sad Steps', the sun in 'Solar' seems to be a source of unquestionable good and generosity, as it is in 'High Windows', which ends with a spiritual vision of the 'endless' skies. In 'Sad Steps' the moon is apostrophised as 'Lozenge of love! Medallion of art!' which emphasises its physical beauty and its divine properties. It is also, however, a thing

of 'hardness' and 'pain/Far-reaching singleness', which suggests a less comforting power.

- In 'The Explosion' the sun under which the slagheaps have slept peacefully is 'dimmed' by the dust of the detonation, suggesting grief and death.
- The sun is not always an unambiguous force, however. In 'Money' the sun contributes to the 'mad' appearance of the churches in the final stanza.
- The moon appears in 'Vers de Société' as a threatening 'air-sharpened blade'. The reduction of the moon to a sliver reflects how reduced life is for the persona.

Light and dark

Light and dark appear in many poems and are frequently linked to the heavenly bodies discussed above, as sources or reflectors of natural light. Larkin often refers to artificial light too. It contrasts with the natural light the collection explores in poems such as 'To the Sea', 'Sad Steps', 'Solar' and 'High Windows'. Unnatural light is often more threatening and suggests the claustrophobia of human existence. Key examples are found in the following poems:

- 'Livings I' — cigarette smoke hangs against the electric light of the bar. It helps create a sense of an enclosed and dim place, a symbol of the passing world from which the persona at the end of the poem decides to escape.
- 'Livings II' — this poem takes place on a lighthouse, a source of manmade light. While the good intentions of this light are clear — seeking to save lives — it is linked to loneliness and danger.
- 'Livings III' — 'candleflames' and firelight illuminate this dinner scene, emphasising its primitive and half-civilised nature. The flickering light of the flames captures the motion of the wine-fuelled conversation. The contrast with the clear and pristine light of the sparkling 'Chaldean constellations' at the end of the poem is stark.
- 'Friday Night in the Royal Station Hotel' — the ambiguous nature of the hotel's light is summed up in the oxymoronic opening line: 'Light spreads darkly downwards'. The light seems pointless and empty, capturing the dull and unpeopled weekend business hotel. These lights, like so much in the poem, do not serve to create a sense of life, but to emphasise the lack of it.
- 'The Old Fools' — the 'lighted rooms' inside the heads of the elderly in the third stanza serve to deepen the pathos of the poem. The image suggests a film or the stage, creating the sense of unreality and distance that characterises the existence of the old fools. As in 'Livings III', natural light ('the sun's/Faint friendliness') provides a telling contrast to the light of lamps and fire.
- 'The Card-Players' — firelight ('firelit', 'grate') and the glow of cigars create the sense of darkness and half-seen reality that is essential to the poem. It adds to the dark, elemental forces of the poem but also promises a haven from the clashing storm.

- 'Dublinesque' — the sadness of the funeral is reflected in the dullness of the afternoon, 'Where light is pewter/And afternoon mist/Brings light on in shops'. The burning and ineffective electric light adds to the pathetic atmosphere.
- 'Vers de Société' — the artificial sources of light in this poem (the 'gas fire' of stanza 1 and the lamp of stanzas 3 and 6) create a variety of effects. The gas fire cannot overcome the oppressive image of the trees, which are 'darkly swayed', a threatening presence outside the window reminiscent of the trees in 'The Card-Players'. The lamp in stanza 3 seems to be a source of some comfort, perhaps academic activity. The 'repayment' it promises, however, is a victim of the social demands the poem explores. The lamp in the final stanza could promise fulfilment and 'peace', but instead it brings 'other things' and can only imperfectly keep at bay the 'failure and remorse' that stand beyond.

Wind

Wind appears as a powerful and unsettling force of nature in a number of poems. 'Livings II' displays the fearsome power of the gale and 'Sad Steps' evokes a moment of epiphany under 'a wind-picked sky'. In 'Vers de Société' the wind is a sign of danger and uncertainty outside, and in 'The Card-Players' the wildness of the weather corresponds to the earthy, untamed behaviour of the men.

Flowers and trees

Larkin generally uses flowers to represent beauty and vitality. In 'The Old Fools', 'the million-petalled flower/Of being here' symbolises life itself in all its miraculous and manifold wonder. 'Cut Grass' uses 'chestnut flowers' and 'White lilac' to evoke an idyllic summer; 'Forget What Did' identifies 'The day the flowers come' as one of three events that would be worth recording. In 'Solar', the sun, the endless giver of light and heat, is described as a 'Single stalkless flower' with a 'petalled head of flames'. However, in 'Dublinesque' and 'The Building' flowers are more darkly connected to life through the presence or threat of its obverse, death.

Trees appear in the following poems:
- In 'The Trees', they are a symbol of hope and renewal. Their growth cycle encompasses both death and life, but life is literally ingrained in them. The repetition of 'afresh' and the 'greenness' of stanza 1 are full of promise.
- The 'village louts' of 'Going, Going' climb trees, representing a past and seemingly innocent era. The cutting down of these trees ushers in the suggestion of less innocent pastimes.
- The 'wet century-wide trees' of 'The Card-Players' are an altogether darker image. Still, however, the trees are an image of endurance and solidity.
- 'Homage to a Government' evokes 'tree-muffled squares'. The trees here signify controlled nature, a sign of respectable, unthinking, uncritical order.

Eyes and sight

Watching and being watched are important concepts in *High Windows*. The presence of windows throughout the collection, and the vantage point they provide of the world inside or outside, are closely related to this idea. Significant examples can be found in the following poems:

- 'Forget What Did' — the writer of the diary looks back in a detached and dispassionate way on the events of his past, which he now wishes to forget. He will continue to be an observer, however, watching the movement of the larger forces that govern life, such as 'observed//Celestial recurrences'.

- 'High Windows' — the poem begins with seeing ('When I see a couple of kids') and it is based upon observation and being observed. One generation watches another and evaluates its own position relative to it. The poem ends with visionary, endless vistas of sky and time.

- 'The Old Fools' — the elderly are observed decaying and pathetically 'Watching light move'. The magic lantern imagery of stanza 3 demonstrates the extent to which they are distanced from their own past lives. The final stanza, with its death-mountain, again focuses on seeing. The 'peak' of death is always in view, but it is something that, presumably for self-protection, the old choose not to see ('never perceiving/How near it is').

- 'The Building' — the hospital in this poem is full of nervous, watching eyes. They look for the arrival of porters and nurses and take in their clinical, uncomforting surroundings (e.g. stanza 5). The poem also portrays the fear of what is not seen and known (e.g. the 'unseen congregations' of stanza 8).

- 'Sad Steps' — the ageing persona of this poem finds himself looking out on the moonlit gardens outside his window. He is greeted by the 'hardness and brightness' of the moon's single eye and caught in 'the plain/Far-reaching singleness of that wide stare'. The scrutiny of the moon brings him face to face with the reality of his own ageing. The moon brings him no comfort: instead it dissects his soul.

- 'Solar' — like the moon in 'Sad Steps', the sun resembles a giant single eye in the sky. The poem also considers a range of ways of seeing the sun (e.g. a 'Suspended lion face' or a 'Single stalkless flower'). The importance of seeing is identified in stanza 2 ('The eye sees you').

Horizontals

Many poems in *High Windows* make use of horizontal images. These are sometimes used to suggest breadth and space, which is often absent from the situations in which the poems' personas find themselves. Horizontals usually offer openness instead of constriction, freedom instead of constraint. However, some of the

horizontals in the collection are enclosed, suggesting the claustrophobic confinement of the personas. Significant examples are found in:

- 'To the Sea' — the 'low horizon' is one of the key features of the opening stanza; the rest of the seaside world Larkin presents is defined against it ('Everything crowds under the low horizon'). The horizon represents the young and the old who crowd there, the passage of time the poem traces and the openness of the 'honest', unspoilt holiday the poem represents.
- 'Livings I' — the horizon of the estuary in the final stanza is an image of promise and beauty.
- 'Friday Night in the Royal Station Hotel' — the 'shoeless corridors' of line 10, which are free of people and clutter, make clear how enclosed and isolated the hotel is.
- 'The Card-Players' — the 'century-wide trees' are a temporal horizon against which the experiences of Jan van Hogspeuw and the other characters are to be measured.
- 'The Building' — like those described in 'Friday Night in the Royal Station Hotel', the corridors of the hospital represent the entrapment experienced by the patients. The idea of horizontals is significant in that all the patients in the hospital have been levelled by illness, which is no respecter of class or gender.

Opposites

Opposites appear frequently in *High Windows*. They may reflect Larkin's ambiguous relationship with the world around him and his often uneasy sense of not belonging. You should consider the following sets of opposites in detail and explore the relationships between the opposing elements.

Noise and silence

Silence and noise are concepts that attach readily to a number of the key themes in the collection, such as death and life, isolation and community, and constraint and freedom.

- 'Friday Night in the Royal Station Hotel' — 'silence laid like carpet' suggests a blanketing, muffling, ubiquitous quietness, in contrast to the noise and bustle that is evidently the norm during the week, when the hotel is occupied by salesmen whose cigarette ash still fills the ashtrays.
- 'To the Sea' — we hear 'hushed waves', but also find bathers 'in hearing of the surf', the sound of 'transistors' and 'The distant bathers' weak protesting trebles'.
- 'Sympathy in White Major' — the poem opens with the clink of ice in a glass and the fizz of pouring tonic water; this contrasts with the pervading silence of death.

- 'Livings II' — sounds are important in the evocation of a lighthouse: the 'Radio rubs its legs,/Telling me of elsewhere', rather like a giant grasshopper, while 'The sea explodes' against the rocks at the base of the lighthouse; in 'Livings III' the evening and its buzz of pointless conversation pass away to the repeated chiming of clock bells.
- 'The Old Fools' — the scenes relived in the old people's memories are like silent movies; the persona is disturbed by the old people's silence and quiescence: 'Why aren't they screaming?'
- 'The Card-Players' — the men's fraternity is conveyed through the sounds of their bodily functions, such as snoring, belching and farting; the fragments of love songs suggest a higher plane of human experience, while the sound of the trees outside evokes nature and the wider world.
- 'The Building' — here Larkin evokes the fearful silence of the hospital waiting room.

Past, present and future

Larkin explores the passage of time and its impact upon both individuals and society in a number of poems. The following poems have an individual focus:
- 'The Old Fools' — this poem deals with the changes caused by age and the terrible reality of ageing.
- 'To The Sea' — the world of this poem seems almost timeless.
- 'Forget What Did' — the diary writer wishes to expunge the past; the future will take account of different matters.
- 'Livings I' — the past, summed up in the tired family business, is in need of change, as the last line indicates.
- 'Posterity' — the biographer focuses on his subject's past, aware that the work he does impacts upon his own present and future for 'at least a year'.
- 'Sad Steps' — the lonely walker is brought face to face with the reality of the present and how different things were in the past.

Other poems have a social focus:
- 'High Windows' and 'Annus Mirabilis' — these both deal with how time has wrought changes in social views of sexual relationships.
- 'Going, Going' — this poem explores the physical changes in England and how these reflect new social concerns.
- 'Homage to a Government' — this poem projects into an imaginary future and explores political hypocrisy.
- 'How Distant' — as in 'To the Sea', past, present and future seem to become one in timeless synthesis.
- 'Show Saturday' — the rural show exists on into the present, but seems like a relic of an outdated past, although the voice of the poem wishes it may 'always be there'.

Country and town

Larkin had an evident affection for England's rural heritage, to which the growing urbanisation was a threat.

- 'Show Saturday' — this poem deals with rural tradition; the show is a quaint and innocent survival of the past into the present, which the persona wishes to see preserved.
- 'Going, Going' — Larkin explores the destruction of picturesque rural England by the growing urban sprawl.
- 'Livings I' — the poem describes a dying breed, the travelling rural salesman peddling livestock products.

Isolation and connection

This is one of the most important set of opposites in *High Windows* and appears extensively, no doubt owing to Larkin's own sense of not belonging.

- 'Vers de Société' — the poem explores in detail the contrast between loneliness and social engagement. The central figure of the poem observes: 'Funny how hard it is to be alone'; this introduces the reader to the pressures of a society that adheres to the rules that '*All solitude is selfish*' and '*Virtue is social*'. On the other hand, we are presented with some images of isolation, for example the hermit of stanza 4, and the young, of whom the speaker observes enviously: 'Only the young can be alone freely.'
- 'The Old Fools' — here Larkin explores isolation from the past, from the body and from the mind. The poem depicts a profound dislocation — personal, social and psychological — that is summed up in the observation that the aged are pathetically 'trying to be there/Yet being here'.
- 'How Distant' and 'Dublinesque' — both these poems explore the corporate experience of isolation; 'Dublinesque' allows the reader a tender insight into the power of personal loss within the collective ritual of the funeral; 'How Distant' similarly evokes a sense of time or life passing, caught not in the voice of a mourner, but in the figure of the girl.
- 'This Be The Verse' — the poem cynically advocates isolation: 'don't have any kids yourself.'
- 'The Building' — isolation is the lot of all the patients, evident in the use of 'all', 'them', 'their' and 'these'; the hospital world is separated from the surrounding workaday world; the patients are 'beyond the stretch/Of any hand from here'.
- 'Friday Night in the Royal Station Hotel' — phrases such as 'letters of exile', 'A larger loneliness' and 'How/Isolated, like a fort, it is' illustrate the disconnection and separation associated with the hotel.
- 'To the Sea' — this poem explores the collective and timeless experience of the British seaside holiday.

- Personal isolation is experienced by many of the characters in the poems, e.g. 'Sad Steps', 'High Windows', 'Forget What Did', 'Livings'.

Freedom and constraint

These are central motifs in Larkin's verse and fiction. Their repeated presence questions the extent to which humans are in fact free, and to what extent they are constrained by their circumstances.

- 'To the Sea' — this poem contrasts words such as 'habit' and 'yearly', which imply routine and cycle, with the evident enjoyment and freedom of the holiday.
- 'How Distant' — this is a poem of escapism and naive hopefulness; the image of the girl 'ramifies endlessly', with an extraordinarily liberating effect.
- 'This Be The Verse' — here freedom is envisaged negatively as the lack of children.
- 'Sad Steps' and 'The Old Fools' study the limitations of age and its effects on the freedom of the mind and the body.

Humour

Larkin's poetry often includes **black** and satirical **humour**. Poems where this is particularly evident, and examples of their humour, are given below.

'Sympathy in White Major'
- The title is a musical joke (e.g. symphony in G major).
- The first stanza is carefree and playful.
- The rhythm is tripping and flippant, belying the seriousness of the occasion.
- It offers a trite summing up of life.
- There is a final dismissal of white and a resultant belittling of the life of the deceased.

'The Card-Players'
- 'The Card-Players' presumably refers to one or more famous paintings of that name by Dutch painters, such as that by Pieter de Hooch (1629–84). It is therefore satirical of the orderly and artificial world they present, as well as a depiction of another, simpler, time when caring about manners and social expectations was not an issue.
- The names of the characters are puns: Hogspeuw is hog's spew; Dogstoerd is dog's turd; Prijck is prick.
- It includes base bodily humour such as belching and farting.

'Posterity'
- Balokowsky is a pun ('bollock-off-sky').
- There is a comic deflation of the biographical subject's life — he is '"One of those old-type *natural* fouled-up guys"'.
- The tone is flippant and dismissive.

'Homage to a Government'

- The poem gives a blackly funny view of political processes, political thought and the justification for policy reversal.
- The repetition of the phrase 'is all right', which implies the opposite, is comic.
- There is a comic distancing from decisions and the blame for decisions.

'This Be The Verse'

- There is a pun on 'fuck you up': it can mean to procreate or to damage.
- The rhythm is tripping and the **rhyme** almost trite.
- The sense of generational repetition and inevitability is comic.
- The poem ends with sardonic 'advice'.

'Annus Mirabilis'

- The repetition of the parenthetical 'Which was rather late for me' is humorous.
- The stanza form and the rhyme scheme are lurching.

'Money'

- Life is cynically reduced to sex and consumer goods.
- The poem includes slang (e.g. 'screw' instead of money).
- The inevitability of failure is comic.

The key poems

'To the Sea'

Linguistic features

Sibilants ('s' sounds)

The repeated use of sibilants throughout the poem reflects the sounds of the sea and the breaking waves upon the beach. Examples include: 'A white steamer stuck'; 'my parents, listeners/To the same seaside quack'; 'The rocks, the rusting soup-tins'.

Long vowel sounds

The poem is full of long vowel sounds (e.g. 'To lie, eat, sleep in hearing of the surf'). These reflect the spacious setting, the atmosphere of ease and leisure, and the vistas of memory that are opened by the visit.

The elements

The presence of all four elements (i.e. water, earth, air and fire) suggests harmony and balance, ideas appropriate to the sunny completeness and positivity of the poem. Water appears throughout, in the 'surf', the 'hushed waves' and the 'clear water'; Earth, or the land, features in the 'steep beach', 'yellow sand' and rocks; air, or

wind, appears in the 'enormous air' and the 'breathed-on glass'; fire is represented in the 'sunlight' of the final stanza.

Memory

Memory is important throughout *High Windows*. As the first poem in the collection, 'To the Sea' initiates Larkin's treatment of this theme.

Personal memory

The opening three lines encapsulate an act of memory: 'To step over the low wall that divides/Road from concrete walk above the shore/Brings back sharply something known long before —'. The physical act of crossing the wall breaks through the boundary between past and present. In stanza 3 the persona reflects overtly on the past: 'happy at being on my own,/I searched the sand for Famous Cricketers,/Or, farther back, my parents'.

Social memory

The poem deals with an enduring aspect of collective English life, the traditional seaside holiday. The annual period of leisure by the sea seems valued by the persona for bringing together old and young and for creating continuity from one generation to the next.

Cycle and routine

Cycle and routine are key themes in 'To the Sea'. The visit to the seaside is 'half an annual pleasure, half a rite', and the first three lines make it clear that the persona is returning to a place where he has been before. At the beginning of stanza 2 he remarks that seaside holidays are 'still going on…still going on!' This continuity is seen in his comment that his parents were 'listeners/To the same seaside quack'.

Other images of cycle and routine include the movement of the sea itself ('The small hushed waves' repeated fresh collapse/Up the warm yellow sand'); the children in stanza 2 being led 'gently up and down'; and the way 'The rigid old' are 'wheel[ed]…along'.

As the poem draws to its conclusion the persona reflects on the value of routine: 'It may be that through habit these do best,/Coming to water clumsily undressed/Yearly'. Note the pun in the word 'habit' on the ideas of customary behaviour and seaside clothing.

Form and style

Rhyme

Larkin employs a complex rhyme scheme for the poem. The repeated ABBACDDEC of the first three stanzas serves to mirror the repeated cycle of seaside holidays. Note that the single, unrhymed, penultimate line of these three stanzas (E) rhymes with the second and third lines of the succeeding stanza. This demonstrates that the poem is not merely cyclical but also has a linear progression. The rhyme scheme is varied in the final stanza to end with a couplet. This lends finality to the poem and adds to its affirmative emphasis on shared values and shared experience.

Enjambement

This is a recurring feature in the poem, both across line endings and across stanzas. The flow of language mirrors the tides and the fluid movement of the sea. It reflects the easy repetition and cycle that are at the conceptual heart of the poem.

Syntax

The syntax of this poem varies widely, from the short simplicity of the two sentences that open the final stanza to the long sentences and multiple subordinations of stanzas 2, 3 and 4. The syntactical ebb and flow of the sentences mirrors the ebb and flow of the tides.

Seaside holidays

This poem presents an idyllic view of the English seaside holiday. It paints a colourful picture of pleasure and relaxation in what seems a quaint and old-fashioned but still important fixture in the social calendar. The traditional seaside activities are inherently humanising, but the idea that the holiday is 'half a rite' gives it a quasi-religious significance.

'High Windows' and 'Annus Mirabilis'

One of Larkin's most famous poems, no doubt in part owing to its use of obscenities, 'High Windows' is the title poem and its themes are central to the rest of the collection. 'Annus Mirabilis' can be seen as a companion piece, since it too deals with issues of sexuality and explores social and moral change.

The narrative voice in these poems has often been associated with Larkin's own, but given Larkin's relatively active sex life and his predilection for pornography this interpretation seems untenable. As with other poems, it is more fruitful to regard the persona as a literary creation with an identity separate from the poet's.

Social change

The 1960s was a period of considerable social change (see pp. 20–22), and this is reflected in 'High Windows' and 'Annus Mirabilis'. New attitudes towards religion are referred to in 'High Windows' with the observation that fear of the priest and God is no longer prevalent in society. The rise of popular music, as epitomised by the advent of the Beatles, is one of the defining features of the new age in 'Annus Mirabilis'.

Sexual behaviour

The change probably most evident in 'High Windows' and 'Annus Mirabilis' is the liberalisation of attitudes towards sexual behaviour. This was accompanied by a relaxing of literary censorship, exemplified in the lifting of the ban on D. H. Lawrence's most controversial novel, *Lady Chatterley's Lover*, in 1963 — an event alluded to in 'Annus Mirabilis'. It had been banned for 35 years for its overt, and what was then considered obscene, presentation of sexual relations.

The persona of 'High Windows' feels enviously excluded from the 'paradise' of sexual freedom that is open to the younger generation and the persona of 'Annus Mirabilis' feels that he missed the boat as far as sex without marriage is concerned; in his youth, sexual relations always involved a 'wrangle for a ring'. In contrast, Larkin had several sexual relationships outside marriage, and these began long before 1963. They did not bring him the happiness that the young people enjoy, however, and his inability to make a permanent commitment through marriage caused him feelings of guilt.

Larkin was a prolific collector of pornography and 'High Windows' begins with a voyeuristic imagining of a passing young couple having sex.

Opposites

The poems achieve some of their effects by setting up the following pairs of opposites.

Narrowness and breadth

The poems deal with moral standpoints. The 'narrow' views of the past are contrasted with the more open and relaxed attitudes of the present. The constrictive vocabulary of 'Annus Mirabilis' (e.g. 'ban', 'wrangle', 'bargaining', 'shame') can be compared to the more expansive vocabulary and syntax of 'High Windows' (e.g. the long opening sentence, the use of sexual language such as 'fucking' and 'diaphragm').

Freedom and constraint

The sexual reserve and anxiety of the men in both poems are evident. The parenthetical 'rather late for me' suggests that the narrator of 'Annus Mirabilis' does not share in the new-found liberties of 1963 and does not benefit from the 'brilliant breaking of the bank' experienced by society in general. Similarly, in 'High Windows' we sense that the voyeur/narrator does not himself have access to the 'paradise' of the young, sexually active couple he watches. Both men seem to fall between the stools of restraint and freedom.

Individual and community

Both poems deal with an individual who is out of step with the prevailing views of his society. In both poems he appears to be an outsider.

Public and private

The formerly private and unmentionable issue of sexual relations has become an open subject for discussion. The personas in both poems, however, evidently find it difficult to convey their personal feelings, a symptom of their innate reserve on the topic of sex. The wordlessness of 'High Windows' may represent a move towards intellectualism and abstraction, a respresentation of the huge vistas of sky with which the poem ends. The humorous tone of 'Annus Mirabilis' may be a satirical response to the idea that such sexual liberation in fact represents anything particularly new or marvellous.

Cyclical and linear

'High Windows' presents both a cyclical view of generational change and a linear view of developing attitudes (see in particular the image of the slide). 'Annus Mirabilis' is cyclical in form (see its use of repetition in the opening and closing stanzas), but also emphasises a linear change in society's views.

'The Old Fools'

In common with much of Larkin's poetry, this poem elicits radically different emotional responses. Draper comments:

> The poem's progress is one of deepening attention, moving from a seemingly detached, jeering stance…to an increasingly sympathetic identification with the subject of senile decay.
>
> (*An Introduction to Twentieth-Century Poetry in English*, Macmillan, 1999)

Booth, on the other hand, sees in the poem 'an embarrassingly obvious displaced terror of death' (*Philip Larkin: Writer*, Harvester Wheatsheaf, 1992). The 'hideous inverted childhood' Larkin presents in this poem relates interestingly to his dislike of children, as well as the collection's concern with cycles and repetition.

Change and decay

Change and decay are key themes in 'The Old Fools', as is reflected in the opening lines: 'What do they think has happened, the old fools,/To make them like this?' As the brutal title suggests, Larkin addresses the experience of ageing with scrupulous, harsh honesty. The relentless rhetorical questions in the first stanza establish a note of interrogation which culminates with 'Why aren't they screaming?' — summing up the persona's frustrated incomprehension at the old people's apparent acquiescence.

The table below identifies examples of change and decay in the poem.

Change or decay of the body and the faculties	Change or decay of the mind
'mouth hangs open and drools'	'can't remember/Who called this morning'
'pissing' themselves	'not knowing how'
'not hearing who'	'the power/Of choosing gone'
'Ash hair, toad hands, prune face dried into lines'	'People you know, yet can't quite name'
'the constant wear and tear/Of taken breath'	'An air of baffled absence'
'hideous inverted childhood'	'hideous inverted childhood'

Death

Death is close in this poem as the old people come towards the end of their lives. The poem charts the beginnings of death even within life — 'the old fools' are steadily losing their grip on the state of living. Larkin describes how 'At death, you break up: the bits that were you/Start speeding away from each other for ever'; this reflects the fragmentation of the body and suggests the separation of body and soul — the description could be said to apply to ageing too.

The elderly are in the thrall of 'Extinction's alp', 'The peak that stays in view wherever we go'. This metaphor suggests that death is an ever-present part of life, always visible. To 'the old fools', however, it is a reality they have begun to approach. Continuing the metaphor, for them death 'is rising ground' — they are on its foothills.

The poem ends by underlining the inevitability of death for all of us: 'Well,/We shall find out.' This is the delayed and unconsoling answer to all the questions the poem has raised.

Past and present

As might be expected in a poem about ageing and death, emphasis is placed on the relationship between past and present. Connected to this is a strong sense of loss. The opening question, 'What do they think has happened, the old fools,/To make them like this?', establishes that with the passage of time the elderly people have changed: they are different in the present from how they were in the past. The use of the phrase 'old fools' to designate them in their present condition conveys that this change is not for the better. 'Do they somehow suppose/...that, if they only chose,/They could alter things back to when they danced all night' underlines that time is irreversible and the past cannot be recovered. The next line mentions specific experiences (of getting married or going to war) that point up the contrast between the old people's busy, active past and their empty, vacant present.

The old people live in the past ('That is where they live:/Not here and now, but where all happened once'), and this is what makes them seem confused and far away: 'trying to be there/Yet being here.' Remembering people from the past is a reminder of what has been lost: 'each looms/Like a deep loss restored'.

Memory

Memory is one of the major themes of *High Windows* and plays a significant role in 'The Old Fools'. Short-term memory loss is the first memory function mentioned in the poem: the old people 'can't remember/Who called this morning'. The vague references to familiarity ('People you know'; 'known doors'; 'known book') highlight the imperfect operation of memory, which recovers only part of what the old people once knew. Already incomplete, the old people's memories are growing fainter: 'the rooms grow farther'.

In 'each looms/Like a deep loss restored', the word 'restored' suggests that memory can bring lost people back, but it can also be read as meaning that to remember is to experience the loss anew. The word 'looms' has hallucinatory overtones, evoking the distortion sometimes worked by memory and the disproportionate significance it can give to things.

'To the Sea' also deals with issues of memory, both personal and collective, and the relationship between youth and age, considering the ways in which memories and experience are passed down. 'Forget What Did' deals with the conscious decision to obliterate memory, in contrast with the undesired forgetfulness of senility.

Imagery

Light and dark

The 'old fools' sit 'Watching light move' — the slowness of the movement of light, and the futility of following its progress, highlight the pathos of the old people's existence. The activity conjures up an image of the old people as being in a trance-like state, lost in their daydreams, and watching the light without really seeing it.

The observation that 'Perhaps being old is having lighted rooms/Inside your head' suggests a kind of magic lantern show of the past. One of the recollected figures in this show is seen 'Setting down a lamp', but the illumination this implies is imperfect: the identities of all the people from the past remain mysterious. Later the human figures are absent from the old people's reminiscences. The images of light grow more impersonal: 'a fire burning' and 'the sun's/Faint friendliness on the wall'. There is some warmth and comfort in these images, but it is diminished by our awareness that the fire and the sun are only memories.

Towards the end of the poem, night is represented as a time when the old are visited by 'strangers' in the dark. Again, these figures have no material existence, but live inside their heads like demons, embodying their fears about death. This image

of night contrasts with the memory described in stanza 1 of dancing all night at a time when there was vitality and romance in the elderly's lives.

The body

The poem deals with the failure of the body and its functions. Stanza 1 creates a pathetic picture of drooling, incontinent elderly people, their mouths foolishly agape, moving as if 'crippled' or 'tight' (i.e. drunk). Their physical state is sharply in contrast to their vitality in youth, when they danced or 'sloped arms' (i.e. joined the military). Stanza 2 captures the decay of the body, presenting it as a literal breaking up or fragmentation. The 'toad hands, prune face' of the penultimate line evokes hideously wrinkled and desiccated body parts, while 'Ash hair' alludes to future cremation as well as evoking greyish-whiteness. In stanza 4, even the basic function of breathing is represented as contributing to the 'constant wear and tear' on the body.

Mountains

Two powerful images of mountains appear in the final stanza of the poem. 'Extinction's alp' suggests the enormity, awesomeness and indomitability of death, as well as evoking danger. 'The peak that stays in view wherever we go' conveys the ubiquity and inescapability of death. For the elderly, death is 'rising ground' — they are forced to recognise that they are on its ascending slopes.

'Going, Going'

This poem is about the changing face of England and Englishness. The title brings to mind the auction room and its catchphrase, 'Going, going, gone'. This provides a number of useful ideas for understanding the poem. The metaphor of the auction could imply that the country is a commodity which is being sold to the highest bidder — the sale will result in the disappearance of traditional England, as suggested by the withheld 'gone'. The idea of competing against other bidders creates a sense of momentum and drive. The inevitability of the process of loss the poem traces is conveyed by the need to complete the cliché that forms the title.

National character

The table below gives characteristics of the 'old' England and the 'new' England presented in the poem.

'Old' England	'New' England
fields	split-level shopping
farms	bleak high-risers
village louts	filth in the sea
trees to climb	M1 café

'Old' England	'New' England
old streets	more houses
unspoilt dales	more parking
shadows	more caravan sites
meadows	concrete
lanes	tyres
guildhalls	rubbish
carved choir stalls in churches	

The persona's feelings in response to the changes he perceives are complex. The opening line of the poem establishes a nostalgic tone: 'I thought it would last my time'; the persona recreates an idyllic picture of rural England, with its quaint lanes, churches and rolling fields. But some of the vocabulary, such as 'crooks', 'tarts', 'the whole/Boiling' indicates anger. The parenthetical comments — '(and ten/Per cent more in the estuaries)', '(Grey area grants!)' — cynically identify the profit motive as the engine behind change. The poem ends on a tone of resigned sadness, accepting that change is imminent and inevitable: 'it will happen, soon.'

Speed

Speed is an important motif in the poem. Vocabulary relating to speed creates a sense of the growing pace at which old England is passing away and evokes ideas of relentless advance and inevitability:

- The M1 is an embodiment of the speed of the new age.
- The formula 'More...more.../More...more...' suggests gathering momentum.
- The **ellipsis** in stanza 6 suggests that there is scarcely even time to complete a thought before it has been taken away.
- The persona is dismayed that change is 'happening so very fast'.
- England is foreseen as becoming the 'First slum of Europe', as if others are speedily headed that way too.
- The persona's final observation that 'it will happen, soon', underlines the sense of imminence. Verbs such as 'last' (stanza 6) and 'linger' (stanza 8) only accentuate the persona's feelings of powerlessness to prevent rapid change.

Consumerism and business

Consumerism and business are key concerns in 'Going, Going', reflecting the changing nature of English culture in the 1960s and early 1970s. The persona sees consumerism and business as both symbols and causes of the destructive progress he laments. This destruction is linked to a change in society's attitudes. The seemingly innocent and benign 'village louts' of the first stanza, who can find nothing worse to do with their time than climb trees, are replaced by the screaming and demanding horde of children in the motorway café. The 'old streets' of the town with their small family businesses and quaint shops are replaced by impersonal and characterless 'split-level shopping'. Businessmen are presented as smug and greedy figures concerned only with money and profit, even where this is bought at the expense of the environment and their cultural heritage.

Destruction

Destruction and spoiling feature repeatedly in 'Going, Going'.

- The poem begins with implied destruction: 'I thought it would last my time'.
- The destruction of trees ends the innocent diversions of the 'village louts'.
- The 'bleak high-risers' are **personified**; they are made the subjects of an active verb, 'come', as if they wreak destruction of their own volition.
- Humans 'mess [the environment] about' in stanza 3, polluting the sea.
- The envisaged slums imply that redevelopment is spoiling not only the built heritage but also the social fabric.

Opposites

Town and country

The assumption that 'beyond the town,/There would always be fields and farms' is challenged in the poem; the expansion of towns and industry is eating up the unspoilt dales, the estuaries, the trees and 'all the land left free'.

Filth and cleanness

The greenness of trees, meadows and dales is replaced by the greyness of industry; the clean tides and estuaries are sullied by 'filth' and industrial waste; the streets are envisaged filled with 'garbage'.

More and less

The poem presents the country as being in disequilibrium because of the imbalance between what there is more of and what there is less of; the children in stanza 4 demand 'More...more.../More...more...'; the businessmen are after ever more profit, entailing more destruction of the countryside; and all of this means that less and less remains of the England the persona wishes to see preserved.

Objects and people

The persona points to the resilience of some historical aspects of England such as 'old streets'; 'Things are tougher than we are', but the poem implies that modern substances and commodities such as brick, concrete, rubbish and tyres are obliterating the rural and historic environments. The insatiable consumer appetite for objects entails relentless destruction of the natural world and the traditions that the persona associates with it; old England is envisaged surviving only in the form of relatively lifeless objects such as 'books' and paintings in 'galleries'.

Motorways and country lanes

The lanes represent the gentle pace and idyllic ease of the past, while the M1 encapsulates the impersonality and speed of the new England.

New buildings and old buildings

The 'high-risers', 'split-level shopping' and new houses of modern England contrast to the 'old streets', 'guildhalls' and church 'choirs' of the old, and the persona fears that the country will become so overdeveloped ('bricked in') that it will turn into a slum.

'The Building'

The prominence and significance of the hospital building are immediately established and are emphasised throughout the poem. The title itself, with its use of the definite article (*the* building), creates the sense that this is an important place. By not specifying the type of building, however, it has a menacing effect. It takes the reader some time to realise that this is a hospital. Even though the building stands in the heart of the town (near busy roads, a church and 'short terraced streets'), it is at once set apart and noticeably different from everything else around it: 'Higher than the handsomest hotel/The lucent comb shows up for miles'. This establishes its physical dominance and psychological power. In the final stanza it is described as 'This clean-sliced cliff', an image which combines the notion of clinical cleanliness with the idea of something uncompromising and unscalable — a precipice off which we are all destined to fall in the end.

The physical stature and solidity of the building create an impression of something powerful and forbidding, which in turn suggests invincible death. Details about individual parts of the building are mentioned: corridors, doors, rooms, levels, height, windows, lagged pipes, floors, red brick. This evokes clinical dissection, a laying bare of organs and innards, again underlining the mutability and mortality of the human body.

Effects of the building

Larkin describes the building as 'ground curiously neutral', signifying that the hospital levels human experience. Illness has no interest in individual identities, which fall away when people enter hospital: 'homes and names/Suddenly in abeyance'. All distinctions between people collapse in hospital. The gender and age of patients is irrelevant: 'women, men;/Old, young; crude facets of the only coin//This place accepts'. Human life is the payment demanded for the hospital's services, and this is a currency common to us all. These factors contribute to the sense of the hospital as impersonal, but the emotions of the patients entering the hospital, and the influence of the place on its surroundings, are presented in a far from neutral light.

The building has a considerable effect on the patients. Their 'nervous eyes' convey the fear that is commonly experienced in hospital. They are 'quiet', as if speech is inappropriate and inadequate, and sit 'tamely', as if their spirit and will have been taken away by the place and what it represents. They are both 'restless and resigned', which demonstrates the paradoxical nature of the patients' emotions. The patients know their fate is inescapable but are nonetheless nervous in the face of it. They display their nerves in a number of ways, by fiddling with teacups, coughing, glancing around, dropping their gloves, and so on. Although collectively undergoing an experience that must sooner or later come to us all, the patients display their own personal forms of discomfort. They nervously and self-consciously watch each other: 'see, as they climb//To their appointed levels, how their eyes/Go to each other, guessing'. This suggests a mixture of sympathy and curious specula-tion about each other's illnesses. It also hints at the tendency people have to try to divine their own fates from what is happening to others.

The patients are 'Here to confess', as if their illness is a sin or venial weakness for which they need to be forgiven. On the other hand, what they have come to confess is that 'something has gone wrong', which suggests that the fault lies not with them but somewhere beyond their control.

The nursing staff is described in very different terms and adds to, rather than alleviates, the atmosphere of uneasiness. Unlike the patients, who have been 'picked out of' their working lives, this is business as usual for the nurses, as is expressed by the clockwork fashion in which they summon the patients: 'Every few minutes comes a kind of nurse/To fetch someone away'. The phrase 'kind of nurse' suggests incomprehension and uncertainty on the part of the patients. Instead of designating a '*kind* nurse' it shows us someone more questionable — a 'kind *of* nurse'. Later in the poem, the nurse's wordless gesture of beckoning a patient is unnerving, as if summoning the person concerned to an unspeakable fate.

Cycles and routines

The poem is concerned with the grand cycle of life and death, but there are also several references to recurrence on a smaller scale. The fact that a nurse comes 'Every few minutes' suggests that illness and death strike at regular intervals. There is a similar sense of timekeeping and clockwork behind the periodic arrival of new patients: 'what keep drawing up/At the entrance are not taxis'. The images of the airport lounge and the bus in stanza 2 suggest schedules and timetables as do the visitors who come with their pointless offerings 'each evening'.

Set against the idea of cycle and routine, however, is a rather different impulse. The normal weekday routine has been broken for the people who have had to go to hospital: it is 'Half-past eleven on a working day' but they have been 'picked out of it'. Coming soon after a reference to 'time', this phrase suggests that the patients have been plucked out of life itself. The idea of being 'picked out' also implies that they have been selected or singled out for misfortune. Linear images such as the hospital corridors emphasise that all human beings are on an unrepeatable course directed towards death. This is also suggested by the series of rooms described in stanza 5: 'For past these doors are rooms, and rooms past those,/And more rooms yet, each one further off//And harder to return from'.

Death and illness

Death and illness are central preoccupations in this poem, as they are elsewhere in the collection. Healthy and unhealthy states are represented as wholly divided from one another, with no possibility for the unwell to regain access to normal, carefree life: 'O world,/Your loves, your chances, are beyond the stretch/Of any hand from here!' Death is universal — 'All know they are going to die'— and eventually all are made conscious of the frailty of their body: 'conceits/And self-protecting ignorance congeal/To carry life, collapsing only when//Called to these corridors.'

Death is never really out of sight. The description of the hospital, which stands for death, being visible for miles around recalls the metaphor for death in 'The Old Fools', 'The peak that stays in view wherever we go'.

Opposites

The table below identifies sets of opposites employed in the poem and explores their effect.

Opposites	Examples and effect
Life and death	Life is summed up as 'conceits/And self-protecting ignorance' – wilful self-deceptions intended to avoid acknowledging our mortality. Eventually, however, the prospect of death has to be faced: 'All know they are going to die.'
Health and sickness	The hospital (representing sickness) is a world apart from the city outside (which represents health). The 'frightening smell' of illness and death hangs over the building, and entering it is a confession that the body is failing: 'something has gone wrong'. The sick people in the hospital are represented as having lost hope and the power of choice.
Staff, visitors and patients	The poem makes a clear distinction between nurses and visitors on the one hand and patients on the other. Visitors are powerless to help their relatives (the flowers they bring are 'wasteful' and 'weak'), while the nursing staff seem almost threatening (they appear periodically 'to fetch someone away').
Personal and impersonal	The hospital is 'ground curiously neutral', a place where people's individual identities are 'suddenly in abeyance'. 'Like an airport lounge', it is a faceless, utilitarian environment for people in figurative transit, disconnected from their normal lives and relationships. The nature of illness, however, is deeply personal, as is suggested by the idea of confession (stanza 4).

Opposites	Examples and effect
Dream and reality	The outside world seems like a 'touching dream' from which the sick have been rudely awakened by their illness. The experience of being in hospital is represented as a kind of surreal nightmare, with nurses beckoning, people being wheeled around, and faceless, silent masses of the sick lurking indefinitely around.
Inside and outside	The hospital, with its many corridors, seems to go deeper and deeper into itself ('past these doors are rooms, and rooms past those,/And more rooms yet, each one further off//And harder to return from'), while the outside world seems distant and inacces-sible: 'beyond the stretch/Of any hand'. Windows, and the barrier and point of contact they provide between the interior and exterior are also significant.
Freedom and constraint	People outside the hospital freely pursue their daily business, while those inside seem physically and psychologically constrained, as if their autonomy of action and choice-making has been taken from them.

Imagery

The following are all key images with relevance to the broader issues raised by the poem.

Clothing

Clothing imagery is used to create distance between the inside of the hospital and the outside, the healthy and the unwell. Normality and the everyday life from which these patients have come is suggested by 'outdoor clothes'; 'dropped gloves' implies nervousness. The phrase 'washed-to-rags ward clothes' evokes prison clothing. Neither the patients nor prisoners are free to do as they wish or go where they would like. 'Their separates from the cleaners' suggests a luxury and sexuality absent from the building.

Religion

The patients are described as 'all//Here to confess that something has gone wrong'. The word 'confess' is normally associated with sin, but the phrase 'something has gone wrong' suggests an error in the system, as if illness is an aberration. In the hospital wards the patients are 'The unseen congregations whose white rows/Lie set apart above' — an image that associates them with the dead in heaven and implies rows of tombstones.

A 'locked church' is one of the features of the urban landscape near the hospital. This suggests a lack of trust and implies that religious consolation is inaccessible in its vicinity. In the final stanza, visitors bearing 'propitiatory' offerings of flowers come to the hospital as if to a place of religious worship, but their sacrifices are powerless against inevitable death. The persona suggests that medicine would only be able to prevent people dying if it were more powerful than religion: 'unless its powers/Outbuild cathedrals nothing contravenes/The coming dark'.

Transport

There are several references to modes of transport in the poem. The image of the airport lounge is both apt and ironic; it captures the impersonal and functional nature of the waiting room and also indicates that this is only a place people pass through on their way to another destination. The buses imply a simultaneously collective and impersonal experience; the patients are on a shared journey but will join and leave it at different points. The cars passing the hospital are symbols of the freedom unavailable to the people in the hospital. 'At the entrance are not taxis' — ironically, the passengers have the luxury of travelling alone because these are in fact ambulances. As for taxis, you must phone for an ambulance, which will pick you up from wherever you are.

Notes on the other poems

'Sympathy in White Major'

A satirical poem concerning the persona's response to the death of an acquaintance he did not actually like. The repeated use of clichés and platitudes to describe the deceased Major (in italics to show these are comments made by other voices at the funeral), and the trite rhyme and rhythm undermine any suggestion of grief and convey the hypocrisy of the occasion, where the gin and tonic is more memorable than the man. The language is a parody of empty middle-class social talk.

'The Trees'

A typically restrained but wide-reaching lyric, this poem deals with the profound issues of life and death. The trees are an enduring image of the cycle of life within which death plays an integral part, but the message is that humans cannot so easily be born again and begin afresh, and the greenness of the trees evokes a kind of grief in us.

'Livings I'

The title of this group of three poems is ironic, as the characters are not living their lives to the full. In the first, the travelling salesman reflects on his own existence and the history of the family business he has inherited, which deals with farmers. He is old-fashioned (the blanks are reminiscent of eighteenth- and early nineteenth-century novels) and follows a regular routine, but comes to the conclusion that it is time for him to change with the times. However, it is ironic that he should refer to it being 1929, the year of the Wall Street Crash when businesses suffered all over Europe because of unregulated expansion and greed. This poem is typical of Larkin's use of names to root the persona in a social context.

'Livings II'

From the viewpoint of a lighthouse, cut off from society, the persona describes a life of isolation threatened by the elements, which he finds beautiful and exhilarating. The poem contains striking visual and acoustic imagery and use of punctuation for dramatic effect. The final two alliterative lines are memorably condensed and make use of Larkin's recurring image of stratification.

'Livings III'

In the absence of the apparently hypochondriac Master, an all-male dinner at high table in a Cambridge college unfolds. The regular metre and alternate rhyme, and the use of bathos and crude colloquial language such as 'bogs', give the poem a comic air, but this is cancelled by the lofty perspective of the final two lines, which put these intellectual humans into their insignificant historical place. A sizar is a Cambridge undergraduate receiving expenses from college. The Chaldeans were an ancient Mesopotamian civilisation, the point being that the stars have been there from time immemorial and will outlive the self-indulgent pursuits and acquired rights of these smug academics.

This poem has been interpreted as a re-creation of the Last Supper, hence the references to Judas and regicide and the executioner Jack Ketch. These allusions to violent death and betrayal, however, also link to the execution of Charles I (associated with the Cambridge Puritan movement). This would explain the setting of the poem in the past of cobbled streets and log-carrying and chilly studies, though nothing much changed in the environment, hierarchy and ritual of the university between the late seventeenth century and Larkin's time.

'Forget What Did'

The persona decides to give up keeping a diary because he has found it painful to record the scars ('cicatrized') of experience. He does not wish to continue to be controlled by the need to bury his days in a way which spoils them from the moment he awakes ('bleakened waking'), simply by his knowing that he will have to report them in words. He prefers to believe that life is best defined not by the personal but by the larger governing forces of nature — 'Celestial recurrences'.

'Friday Night in the Royal Station Hotel'

The hotel named represents a typical northern station hotel. The sonnet form, normally associated with love, seems ironic given the melancholic and lonely ambience. The poem explores isolation, using contrasting imagery of light and dark, presence and absence. The use of italics at the end of the poem quotes from the kind of compensatory poetic letter travellers exiled in hotels might write. Home versus exile is a common theme in Larkin's work. Like hospitals (and etymologically connected to them), hotels collect unrelated and unwilling inmates and force them to live intimately. There is desolation as well as ambiguity in the word 'shoeless', meaning that few people walk along the corridor, but also that guests no longer bother to put out their shoes for cleaning. The repeated 'l' sound creates an elegiac mood.

'The Card-Players'

'The Card-Players' is the title of a number of well-known paintings. Paul Cézanne (1890–92), Pieter de Hooch (1663–65), Fernand Léger (1917), Rufus Wright (1882) and Lucas van Leyden (c.1520) all produced paintings with this title. Like 'Friday Night in the Royal Station Hotel', this poem adopts the sonnet form. Again, given the decidedly unromantic nature of the poem's content, this seems ironic. The language of the poem is strongly physical, elemental and sometimes scatological. Note the coarse humour in the double entendres of the characters' names, an effect also employed in 'Posterity'. The contrast between dark and light creates a chiaroscuro effect, and Larkin is again using the elements to juxtapose the limited personal and sensual experience with the overarching and unperceived universal one.

'Posterity'

The imagined satirised biographer, Jake Balakowsky (Bollock-off-sky), is a pretentious, trendy, American-Jewish 'wannabe' academic, cheated of his desire to teach in Israel because of his paternal obligations and his wife's family's social aspirations. 'Kennedy' is a catch-all reference to an American university library. He thinks of himself as a radical ('Protest Theater') and is therefore unhappy about being saddled with the 'old-type' guy Larkin. The poem uses the form of a voice-over introducing a dialogue scenario. The colloquial language and rhythm — including run-on stanzas — is counteracted by the three regular stanzas and recurring rhyme.

'Dublinesque'

This poem contains echoes of James Joyce's Dubliners. It describes an Irish funeral, otherwise known as a 'wake', which is paradoxically a celebration. 'Kitty' or 'Katy' are Irish names evocative of 'All love, all beauty'. The juxtaposition of 'race-guides' and 'rosaries' is ironic. This 'air of great friendliness' is in striking contrast to the funeral of the White Major, of whom no one was fond. Larkin found Ireland to be a place where he could be liberated from the social expectations imposed on him in England.

'Homage to a Government'

The title of this poem is clearly satirical, as the prevailing tone of the poem is profoundly critical. Unlike any other poem in the collection, this poem is dated. The year 1969 saw the final withdrawal of British troops from East Suez, an act that signalled the end of the British Empire. The Labour government of the time was led by Harold Wilson, and the foreign secretary was Michael Stewart. Larkin's scathing tone makes clear that this marked a significant turning point in the nation's history and that now 'it's a different country'. The declarative and categorical statements, such as things being 'all right' when they are obviously not, and the repetition of 'Next year', show an unconvincing overconfidence. Larkin is typically attacking the power of money to subvert principle.

'This Be The Verse'

There is a shocking incongruity between the biblical language of the title — from R. L. Stevenson's poem 'Requiem' and used as his epitaph — and the monosyllabic and aggressively colloquial language of the rest of the poem, particularly the first line. The poem betrays Larkin's distrust of marriage and his antipathy to the idea of having children. Parents are criticised for their inconsistent attitudes to discipline in the oxymoron 'soppy-stern', and in the recurring image of layers and shelves the 'misery' of failure is handed down the generations.

'How Distant'

The context is a ship going to Australia carrying young people emigrating in search of a better life, a common postwar phenomenon called 'assisted passage'. The enjambement between the stanzas reflects the movement of the ship. A favourite Larkin image of 'new store clothes' is used to signify youth and modernity (previously clothes were handed down in families or made by tailors and seamstresses, and there were no department stores). The poem shows the progression from leaving the homeland, undertaking the voyage, and arriving in the new world. Streets and other ramifications (such as railway lines) are often used in Larkin's poetry to suggest the dynamism and drama of travel and the process of change.

'Sad Steps'

This poem is an evocation of growing older (compare 'The Old Fools' and 'Vers de Société'). The central image of the watching moon (see other presentations of the heavenly bodies and the celestial in 'Livings II', 'Forget What Did', 'High Windows' and 'Solar'), like a great eye, is both threatening and uncompromising, bringing promise for the young but fear for the ageing persona ('One shivers slightly'). The moon is, however, a thing of beauty and inspiration — compare the Roman view of Diana, goddess of the moon, hunting and love. Once again windows and staring feature as an expression of viewpoint on a different world, one in which celestial and eternal beauty contrasts with physically deteriorating reality on Earth. The word 'immensements' is a pun which links the idea of the moon's constant waxing and waning with the Latin 'mensis', meaning month.

'Solar'

This poem in free verse, which is unusual for Larkin, celebrates the sun by comparing it to a sunflower, a lion's face and mane, haloes, and a gold coin, using diction of abundance and liberality. Again there are 'horizontals' and contrasting images of verticals and climbing to show the movement and freedom of celestial bodies.

'Vers de Société'

Larkin uses Latin and French titles to mock social pretensions or create linguistic contrasts. One has to R.S.V.P. to an invitation, which is what the persona is doing to the satirically named Warlock-Williams. The opening line, as so often, is in a very different idiom of gross informality. The italics are the voices of social clichés and public expressions, and reveal the hypocrisy of 'Playing at goodness' and adopting conformity in what we write to acquaintances, despite what we really think and want to do. The stanza enjambement in this poem creates the effect of an indignant mind in full flow on the injustice of never being allowed to be alone, to enjoy the lamplight of learning and the beauty of the moon. It shows his abhorrence of the tit-for-tat demands of academic partying and the boring pretence of being interested in some 'fool research' or the 'drivel of some bitch'. The ironic progression of the poem is from refusing the invitation to accepting it, because of the fear of 'failure and remorse' and of being labelled selfish and antisocial. The parentheses are typical of Larkin's colloquial and ironic style. Here, as elsewhere, cutlery is used as a symbol of communal eating and social gathering (the persona in 'Livings II' lays the table for one).

'Show Saturday'

This is a celebratory poem, playfully and affectionately exploring the traditional British agricultural fair. The concluding wish that it may 'always be there' suggests the importance of tradition and its innocent enjoyments in a changing world. The use of lists and hyphenated words creates a mood of crowd density, bustling activity and an abundance of sights and sounds. There is a prosaic quality about the line-length, enjambement, and syntax. Compare 'Homage to a Government' and 'Going, Going'.

'Money'

This is another satirical poem in which Larkin attacks contemporary views of money and material possessions. These are seen as the measure of success in life by society, but are ultimately proved to be hollow, and dependence on them 'intensely sad'. Money loses value, even if invested, because the cost of living is always rising. The persona adopts the lofty perspective on money and its slaves through the use of the window image again, which reveals the sad truth of unattractive, commercially driven towns. 'Quarterly' is how often bank statements used to be sent to account holders.

'Cut Grass'

With its focus on the natural world and the interrelations of life and death, this short poem recalls 'The Trees'. The atmosphere of the poem is evocative and celebratory. The monosyllabic diction equates death with the scythe and with whiteness, an archetypal image cluster (see 'Sympathy in White Major'). There is an echo of Seneca's 'ars longa, vita brevis' ('art is long, life is short') in 'Brief is the breath…Long, long the death', evoking a pathos that earthly beauty is vulnerable and ephemeral, but the heavenly clouds can move according to a different time scale, like the stars, sun and moon in other poems. The lyricism of this poem is conveyed largely through the use of the letter 'l'.

'The Explosion'

Set in a County Durham mining community, this poem deals with an explosion down a coalmine and its impact. A mine disaster in 1882 at Trimdon Grange, County Durham, killed 74 miners. A song was written about the explosion, and Larkin admitted he had based his poem upon a song about a real mine explosion. Trimdon has a Wesleyan Methodist chapel. Like many of the poems in the collection, 'The Explosion' juxtaposes life and death, with achingly beautiful images such as the nest of eggs (filled with latent life) and the good humour of the miners contrasting starkly with the death that bursts into their midst. There are allusions to Easter in the eggs, gold haloes, the idea of resurrection and the reference to the tremor at noon. The italics are the platitudinous response of orthodox religion to such an unwarranted act of God. The last line stands alone and the poetry collection ends on a positive note of regeneration.

Extracts from *Jill* and *A Girl in Winter*

These extracts from Larkin's two early novels are notable for their similarities with his later poetry. Capturing the essence of a moment, telling descriptive details and the subtle but pervasive use of opposites — traits which characterise these passages — are typical of the poems in *High Windows*. In the extracts Larkin displays an evident love of the natural world and an ability to convey essential beauty, which are tempered by an aura of melancholy and a fascination with human suffering.

Extract 1: *Jill* (1946)

John Kemp sat in the corner of an empty compartment in a train travelling over the last stretch of line before Oxford. It was nearly four o'clock on a Thursday in the middle of October, and the air had begun to thicken as it always does before a dusk in autumn. The sky had become stiff with opaque clouds. When they were clear of the gasometers, the wagons and blackened bridges of Banbury, he looked out over the fields, noticing the clumps of trees that sped by, whose dying leaves each had an individual colour, from palest ochre to nearly purple, so that each tree stood out distinctly as in spring. The hedges were still green, but the leaves of the convolvuli threaded through them had turned sickly yellow, and from a distance looked like late flowers. Little arms of rivers twisted through the meadows, lined with willows that littered the surface with leaves. The waters were spanned by empty foot-bridges.

It looked cold and deserted. The windows of the carriages were bluish with the swirls of the cleaner's leather still showing on the glass, and he confined his eyes to the compartment. It was a third-class carriage, and the crimson seats smelt of dust and engines and tobacco, but the air was warm. Pictures of Dartmouth Castle and Portmadoc looked at him from the opposite wall. He was an undersized boy, eighteen years old, with a pale face and soft pale hair brushed childishly from left to right. Lying back against the seat, he stretched his legs out and pushed his hands to the bottom of the pockets of his cheap blue overcoat. The lapels of it curled outwards and creases dragged from the buttons. His face was thin, and perhaps strained; the expression round his mouth was ready to become taut, and a small frown lingered on his forehead. His whole appearance lacked luxuriance. Only his silky hair, as soft as seeding thistle, gave him an air of beauty.

Extract 2: *A Girl in Winter*

There had been no more snow during the night, but because the frost continued so that the drifts lay where they had fallen, people told each other there was more to come. And when it grew lighter, it seemed that they were right, for there was no sun, only one vast shell of cloud over the fields and woods. In contrast to the snow the sky looked brown. Indeed, without the snow the morning would have resembled a January nightfall, for what light there was seemed to rise up from it.

It lay in ditches and in hollows in the fields, where only birds walked. In some lanes the wind had swept it up faultlessly to the very tops of the hedges. Villages were cut off until gangs of men could clear a passage on the roads; the labourers could not go out to work, and on the aerodromes near these villages all flying remained cancelled. People who lay ill in bed could see the shine off the ceilings of their rooms, and a puppy confronted with it for the first time howled and crept under the water-butt. The out-houses were roughly powdered down the windward side, the fences were half-submerged like breakwaters; the whole landscape was so white and still it might have been a formal painting. People were unwilling to get up. To look at the snow too long had a hypnotic effect, drawing away all power of concentration, and the cold seemed to cramp the bones, making work harder and unpleasant. Nevertheless, the candles had to be lit, and the ice in the jugs smashed, and the milk unfrozen; the men had to be given their breakfasts and got off to work in the yards. Life had to be carried on, in no matter what circumscribed way; even though one went no further than the window-seat, there was plenty to be done indoors, saved for such time as this.

But through cuttings and along embankments ran the railway lines, and although they were empty, they led on northwards and southwards till they began to join, passing factories that had worked all night, and the backs of houses where light showed round the curtains, reaching the cities where the snow was disregarded, and which the frost could only besiege for a few days, bitterly.

Quotations

Larkin's views and criticism

Larkin's view of himself

To me I seem very much an outsider, yet I suppose 99% of people would say I'm very much establishment and conventional. Funny isn't it?

(quoted in *Philip Larkin: A Writer's Life*, Motion, 1993)

Children

Children are often bored, I think. They don't control their destinies, and they don't do what they want or live where they want.

(Larkin, speaking in a South Bank Show interview with Melvyn Bragg, 1981)

Until I began to meet grown-ups on more or less equal terms I fancied myself a kind of Ishmael. The realisation that it was not people I disliked but children was for me one of those celebrated moments of revelation.

(Larkin, quoted in 'The Savage Seventh' in *Required Writings*, 1983)

Marriage and women

It would be somewhat absurd of me to regret [my father's] marriage, but I could never see why he needed a wife. He liked his own company best and gloried in his ability to look after himself, and his clumsiness in human relations must have made him an unsatisfactory husband, which in turn must have put a certain strain on him. Certainly the marriage left me with two convictions: that human beings should not live together, and that children should be taken from their parents at an early age.

(Larkin, The Philip Larkin Archive, Brynmor Jones Library, Notebook 5)

Fuck all women! I am quite fed up with the whole business: sooner be half full of beer. Sex is designed for people who like overcoming obstacles. I don't like overcoming obstacles.   (Larkin, letter to Kingsley Amis, 22 October 1951)

Poetry

> People say I'm very negative, and I suppose I am, but the impulse for producing a poem is never negative; the most negative poem in the world is a very positive thing to have done.
>
> (Larkin, The Philip Larkin Archive, Brynmor Jones Library, Notebook 4)

> It is sometimes useful to remind ourselves of the simpler aspects of things normally regarded as complicated. Take, for instance, the writing of a poem. It consists of three stages: the first is when a man becomes obsessed with an emotional concept to such a degree that he is compelled to do something about it. What he does is the second stage, namely, construct a verbal device that will reproduce this emotional concept in anyone who cares to read it, anywhere, any time. The third stage is the recurrent situation of people in different times and places setting off the device and re-creating in themselves what the poet felt when he wrote it. The stages are interdependent and all necessary. If there has been no preliminary feeling, the device has nothing to reproduce and the reader will experience nothing. If the second stage has not been well done, the device will not deliver the goods, or will deliver only a few goods to a few people, or will stop delivering them after an absurdly short while. And if there is no third stage, no successful reading, the poem can hardly be said to exist at all.
>
> What a description of this basic structure shows is that poetry is emotional in nature and theatrical in operation, a skilled re-creation of emotion in other people, and that a bad poem is one that never succeeds in doing this. All modes of criticism are no more than different ways of saying this, whatever literary, philosophical or moral terminology they employ, and it would not be necessary to point out anything so obvious if present-day poetry did not suggest that it had been forgotten.
>
> (Larkin, quoted in 'The Pleasure Principle' in *Required Writing*, 1983)

> It is not sufficient to say that poetry has lost its audience, and so need no longer consider it: lots of people still read and even buy poetry. More accurately, poetry has lost its old audience, and gained a new one. This has been caused by the consequences of a cunning merger between poet, literary critic and academic critic (three classes now notoriously indistinguishable): it is hardly an exaggeration to say that the poet has gained the happy position wherein he can praise his own poetry in the press and explain it in the classroom; the reader has been bullied into giving up the consumer's power to say 'I don't like this, bring me something different.'
>
> (Larkin, quoted in 'The Pleasure Principle' in *Required Writing*, 1983)

> The experience of beauty is in Larkin's poetry always in peril and his most lyrically thrilling moments contemplate negation.
>
> (Swarbrick, *Out of Reach: The Poetry of Philip Larkin*, 1995)

[Larkin's poetry] grows out of rage: the rage of unsatisfied desire, the rage of 'shame', the rage of having to persuade everyone that 'the thought of high windows' guarantees happiness.

(Motion, Philip Larkin: A Writer's Life, 1993)

Art

What I don't believe about art is that it should require special knowledge or special training on the part of its consumers. Art is enjoyment, first on the part of the writer, painter or musician, and then, by communication, on the part of the reader and looker and listener.

(Larkin, letter to Steve Race)

From the poems

It is important to learn some useful quotations and think about how you would use them. Make notes on how you could use each of these quotations to support your views on Larkin's poetry.

Brings sharply back something known long before	'To the Sea'
half an annual pleasure, half a rite	ibid.
It may be that through habit these do best	ibid.
Though white is not my favourite colour.	'Sympathy in White Major'
Last year is dead, they seem to say, Begin afresh, afresh, afresh.	'The Trees'
It's time for change, in nineteen twenty-nine.	'Livings I'
Lit shelved liners Grope like mad worlds westward.	'Livings II'
Above, Chaldean constellations Sparkle over crowded roofs.	'Livings III'
Stopping the diary Was a stun to memory	'Forget What Did'
Celestial recurrences	ibid.
I know this is paradise Everyone old has dreamed of all their lives	'High Windows'
Rather than words comes the thought of high windows	ibid.
deep blue air, that shows Nothing, and is nowhere, and is endless.	ibid.

the dining-room declares
A larger loneliness of knives and glass
And silence laid like carpet.   'Friday Night in the Royal Station Hotel'

At death, you break up   'The Old Fools'

Perhaps being old is having lighted rooms
Inside your head, and people in them, acting.   ibid.

The peak that stays in view wherever we go
For them is rising ground.   ibid.

hideous inverted childhood   ibid.

Things are tougher than we are   'Going, Going'

Most things are never meant.   ibid.

Wet century-wide trees
Clash in surrounding starlessness   'The Card-Players'

The secret, bestial peace!   ibid.

that vague age that claims
The end of choice   'The Building'

all
Here to confess that something has gone wrong.   ibid.

O world,
Your loves, your chances, are beyond the stretch
Of any hand from here!   ibid.

nothing contravenes
The coming dark.   ibid.

One of those old-type natural fouled-up guys.   'Posterity'

All we can hope to leave them now is money.   'Homage to a Government'

They fuck you up, your mum and dad.
They may not mean to, but they do.   'This Be The Verse'

Get out as early as you can,
And don't have any kids yourself.   ibid.

the strength and pain
Of being young   'Sad Steps'

Sexual intercourse began
In nineteen sixty-three   'Annus Mirabilis'

Funny how hard it is to be alone.   'Vers de Société'

Only the young can be alone freely.   ibid.

All solitude is selfish.   ibid.

Virtue is social.   ibid.

Beyond the light stand failure and remorse   ibid.

        something they share
That breaks ancestrally each year into
Regenerate union.   'Show Saturday'

I am all you never had of goods and sex.   'Money'

Literary terms and concepts

It is a requirement of Assessment Objective 1 that 'appropriate terminology' be used in written expression relating to texts. The use of literary terms enhances the style and clarity of essays. A familiarity with the terminology also shows an understanding of the traditions, genres and periods of literature. Many of the terms are linked to other arts subjects and help to put literary movements and philosophies in context. Knowing the names for things does more than help us to label them: it draws our attention to the concepts themselves, deepening our awareness and extending our powers of observation. However, knowing the meaning of terms and being able to identify examples of them in texts has no value if you cannot explain the effects they are creating, so beware of scattering unintegrated and uninterpreted terminology in your essays just to try to sound impressive.

Below is a glossary of all the literary terms you are likely to need or to come across during your study of Larkin. You will already know some of them from your previous literary studies and can tick those off immediately; others you will have heard of and can now verify their meaning. As you can see, the majority of these terms are from Greek or Latin, the founding cultures of Western literature, and the rest are French or Italian, so you may be able to guess some of them if you know those languages. It will not be possible to learn all the rest in one go; either your teacher will indicate which are the most useful for the texts you will be studying, or you can learn a few at a time. Adding examples for each, particularly from the texts you are currently studying, is the best way to remember them and to feel confident about using them. The aim is for them to become a natural part of your own spoken and written vocabulary.

alliteration   repetition of initial letter or sound in adjacent words, e.g. 'resurrection,/Regicide and rabbit pie' ('Livings III')

allusion   reference, either direct or indirect, to another text, e.g. 'the *Chatterley* ban' ('Annus Mirabilis')

antithesis   contrast of ideas expressed by setting them against one another

assonance	repetition of vowel sounds in words of close proximity
bathos	descent from the elevated to the commonplace
black humour	humour that makes fun of something serious or sad
caesura	deliberate break or pause in line of poetry, signified by punctuation
cliché	predictable and overused expression or situation, e.g. '*He devoted his life to others*' ('Sympathy in White Major')
colloquialism	informal language of conversational speech
connotations	implications of words and phrases that are over and above their obvious meaning
contextuality	historical, cultural, social, economic and political background of a text
couplet	pair of consecutive rhyming lines
double entendre	expression with two meanings, one of them coarse
ellipsis	omission of word(s) for economy or avoidance of repetition
enjamb(e)ment	run-on line of poetry, usually to reflect its meaning
end-stopped	line that is 'stopped' at the end by a punctuation mark
epiphany	a moment of enlightenment or realisation
feminine ending	a light or unstressed syllable at the end of a line, e.g. 'for ever/endeavour' ('The Old Fools')
hyperbole	deliberate exaggeration for literary effect, e.g. 'rows/of single supreme versions' ('Show Saturday')
imagery	descriptive language appealing to the senses: touch, taste, smell, sight, sound; often creates pictorial or visual effects
internal rhyme	rhyme occurring within a line of poetry
irony	language intended to mean the opposite of the words expressed; amusing or cruel reversal of an outcome expected, intended or deserved; situation in which one is mocked by fate or the facts
juxtaposition	placing ideas, characters, events etc. side by side for (often ironic) contrast or to create other types of literary connection
litotes	an ironical understatement, e.g. 'Though white is not my favourite colour' ('Sympathy in White Major')
metaphor	suppressed comparison which is implied and not stated or literally true, e.g. 'light is pewter' ('Dublinesque')

oxymoron	two contradictory terms united in a single phrase, e.g. 'soppy–stern' ('This Be The Verse')
paradox	seemingly absurd or self-contradictory statement which on reflection contains an element of truth
pathetic fallacy	use of the weather or the landscape to reflect moods, feelings, thoughts etc.
pathos	evocation of pity by a situation of suffering and helplessness, e.g. 'Wives saw men of the explosion//Larger than in life they managed' ('The Explosion')
persona	created voice within a text who plays the role of narrator/speaker
personification	the attribution of human qualities to objects ideas etc.
plurality	possible multiple meanings of a text
pun	use of words with double meaning for humourous or ironic effect
quatrain	a verse that is four lines long, e.g. 'High Windows', 'The Trees' and 'Money'
register	level of formality in expression
rhyme	repetition of final vowel sound in words at the end of lines of poetry
rhythm	pace and sound pattern of writing, created by stress, vowel length, syntax and punctuation
simile	comparison introduced by 'like' or 'as'
sonnet	lyrical poem of 14 lines of rhymed iambic pentameter, e.g. 'The Card-Players'
stereotype	a category of person with typical characteristics, often used for mockery, e.g. the stereotyped businessmen and families of 'Going, Going'
synecdoche	form of metaphor in which a part (often a body part) is used to represent the whole
theme	abstract idea or issue explored in a text
tone	emotional aspect of the voice of a text

Essay questions, specimen plans and notes

The exemplar essay questions which follow can be used for planning practice and/or full essay writing within the time limit, with or without the text. Possible plans are given to show how the titles may be approached. These are suggested responses only and other approaches may be equally valid. Of course, the points identified would need to be illustrated with well-chosen examples and quotations from the text. Accompanying each plan are examiner comments specific to the tasks, which illustrate how the Assessment Objectives are applied by examiners.

Remember to talk about the poem and the persona, not the poet, and try to hear how the poem would sound if read aloud. Form and language are essential elements of poetry, so you must not restrict yourself to a discussion of content. Where appropriate, you may choose to incorporate relevant critical material as a basis for your argument and response.

The question you choose may direct you to one or two prescribed poems or ask you to select your own. Either way you should think about the following:

- Careful selection of poems is crucial to ensure the relevance and success of your essay. The poems you like or are most familiar with are not necessarily the most appropriate for a particular title.
- Show your knowledge of the whole selection as well as your response to and analysis of particular poems.
- Focus closely on the chosen poem(s) but also relate their content and/or language to elsewhere in the selection. Examiners advise that a substantial portion (up to 60%) of responses to passage-based questions should refer to the rest of the work being studied. Link your comments to the overall themes, and suggest ways in which the poem is typical of the poet's work as a whole.
- Don't waste time paraphrasing what happens in a poem; just give a quick summary of its setting and context, noting who is present, where and why.
- Think about reader reaction, using your own as the basis for your response.
- For an open-book exam you will have made annotations in the margin and on the text, but only include the relevant ones, and remember that they need to be organised into a structured response, not just transferred to your essay as a list.

Questions and plans

1 How far do the poems in *High Windows* reflect a disapproving view of money and consumerism? In your answer, you should EITHER refer to TWO or THREE poems in detail OR range more widely through the whole collection.

Possible ideas to include in a plan

- Many of the poems in *High Windows* reflect a deeply sceptical view of the consumer society, which seeks to replace spiritualism with the pursuit of goods or wealth.

- 'Money' portrays the persona's uneasy views about money and its use. Both the currency and the commodities it can purchase, including sex, are seen as debased. The poem's focus on the final image of the french windows suggests that the meaning in life lies above such trivial issues. Money promises everything, but delivers only a feeling of worthlessness and intense sadness.

- 'Money' does, however, point to the important nature of consumerism and the way it affects our perceptions, concluding in stanza 2 that 'Clearly money has something to do with life'. Whether ultimately meaningful or not, humans measure their success in cars and second homes. Money is even allowed a certain attractiveness as the persona listens to it 'singing' like a siren.

- 'Going, Going' exposes the greed that underlies economic progress: businessmen and politicians are eager to sell off the country for development, no matter what the cost in terms of culture, heritage and quality of life. Similarly, the public demand for goods and amenities is represented as a voracious appetite. The old 'certainties' of the poem, like the cathedral cities and country lanes, are being destroyed in the name of so-called progress. The persona sees in the death of such elements of heritage a damning indictment of selfish consumerism.

- Again, however, it can be argued that in 'Going, Going' money and financial gain have their attractions, as the news of a profitable takeover in stanza 5 is met with 'a score/Of spectacled grins'.

- 'Show Saturday' opens a window on a more innocent society through a traditional entertainment in which money is present (the 'pound-note man') but is never seen to dominate. The innocent pastimes at the show and the values they seem to represent, such as community, sharing and rural simplicity, are beyond any price.

- Larkin views social developments and the increasing demand for money and goods with regret and suspicion, seeing in them an essentially hollow attempt to give definition to life.

Examiner comments

Focus: appropriate selection of poems; money and consumerism.

Key phrases: 'How far'; 'disapproving view'; 'money and consumerism'.

AOs 1–3	AO4
■ confident analysis of the poetry	■ thoughtful exploration of the attitude to money and consumerism in the texts
■ cogent argument featuring wide vocabulary	
■ sophisticated and mature	■ insight and originality

The focus for this task is easily established and most candidates should manage to select relevant poems on which to centre their discussion. Typical choices will include 'To the Sea', 'Livings I', 'Going, Going', 'Homage to a Government', 'Annus Mirabilis', 'Show

Saturday' and 'Money'. The prevalence of money and consumer goods in the collection will be identified in all answers, but more advanced responses will go on to consider the way Larkin employs consumer goods and money (and the relationships and equations between them) as a measure of personality and the presence or absence of deeper, spiritual worth. Such responses will also identify the poems' profoundly cynical and questioning view of the value of money and consumer goods in the face of more universal concerns such as death.

Successful candidates will:

- select appropriate poems for this question
- explore the way in which money and consumerism are represented in this collection
- produce a balanced argument in response to the cue in the question 'How far'

Less successful candidates will:

- merely paraphrase their chosen poems
- assert that the poems display Larkin's utter condemnation of money and consumerism
- make simplistic comments about the poems without considering their ambiguities

2 **'One of those old-type *natural* fouled-up guys.' How far is this a fair assessment of the way Larkin presents himself in this collection of poems?**

Possible ideas to include in a plan

- This question draws on a quotation from 'Posterity', in which the biographer Jake Balokowsky reflects on his subject. It suggests the possibility of connecting the views expressed in *High Windows* directly with the views of the poet himself. However, no such straightforward equation between the author and his work is possible. Larkin employs a range of personas and related styles throughout the collection to achieve a variety of effects, and any attempt to directly transfer ideas and views is to over-simplify the nature of the poetry and the poet.
- Many of the views presented by Larkin seem conservative (e.g. 'Show Saturday', 'How Distant') and as such may be considered 'old-type'. This contrasts, however, with the more progressive views expressed about sexual relations ('High Windows' and 'Annus Mirabilis'), though we may question whether Larkin is envious or scathing of new attitudes to sex, which are soulless and impersonal. A love of and a desire to sustain 'old England', its manifestations ('Going, Going') and traditional values ('To the Sea') is evident; a vein of nostalgia emerges as the passing of certain traditional ways of life are considered in 'Show Saturday' and 'Livings I'. However, the extent to which these poems directly reflect Larkin's personal views is open to question.
- What is clearer is Larkin's penchant for presenting characters or personas who are 'fouled up' (e.g. the 'fucked up' progeny of 'This Be The Verse', the desperately introverted writer of 'Forget What Did', the shadowy figures of 'Livings III' and 'The Card-Players'). This displays a fascination with questions surrounding normality

and what may be considered acceptable views. For example, 'Vers de Société' and 'Sympathy in White Major' both look closely at questions of acceptable social behaviour and its impact on the individual, placing the false values of society in contrast to bigger concerns, such as nature and death. Foul language and behaviour in the poems, which reflect questions of social acceptability and norms of behaviour, are relevant too.

■ What is meant by 'natural'? Larkin sees death as a natural state and a natural part of life, exploring it extensively in poems like 'The Old Fools', 'Sad Steps' etc. However, this focus on death and bodily decay may be seen as disturbingly unnatural. Taking on Balokowsky's assertion, it is possible that 'natural' may suggest that his biographical subject is under-theorised. In this respect, the overt rejection of strongly 'theorised' perceptions of literature by the members of the Movement is of interest.

Examiner comments

Focus: Whole text; Larkin's presentation of himself.

Key phrases: 'old-type'; 'natural'; 'fouled-up'; 'fair assessment'; 'himself'.

AOs 1–3	AO4
■ sophisticated analysis of Larkin's style and presentation of himself ■ mastery of text ■ fluent expression with wide vocabulary	■ wide-ranging overview ■ insight and originality

The quotation that provides the starting point for this question is something said by the biographer Jake Balokowsky in 'Posterity'. Some candidates may be distracted by the word 'natural' (focusing on Larkin's attitudes to nature); others may limit themselves to his old-type attitudes in general; some might simplistically assume that Larkin is presenting himself rather than adopting a set of personas. Typical poems for consideration are 'To the Sea', 'Sympathy in White Major', 'Forget What Did', 'High Windows', 'Annus Mirabilis', 'Sad Steps', 'Vers de Société' and 'Posterity'. More astute candidates may equate 'old-type' with 'traditional' and debate the appropriateness of this particular epithet, exploring Larkin's rejection of the postwar values of marriage and family that mark him as unconventional and align him with other members of the Movement.

Successful candidates will:

■ produce relevant and balanced answers addressing all the question's key words, including 'is this a fair assessment'

■ have the mastery to select and detail convincing and relevant examples

■ identify the problems of making unquestioning links between Larkin and his poems

■ analyse Larkin's use of personas to present points of view

■ explore a range of the 'natural' and 'fouled-up' social and personal issues Larkin presents in the collection

Less successful candidates will:

- write about Larkin's attitudes in general, equating these automatically with the views presented in the poems
- choose appropriate examples but not really address the question 'is this a fair assessment?'
- possibly focus on the idea of nature instead of the natural
- show less awareness of the role of personas

Further questions

1 Larkin has been criticised for displaying a lack of sympathy in his poetry. In the light of your reading of *High Windows*, how justifiable do you consider this point of view?

2 'Larkin can sound casual, informal and even coarse, but is essentially a formalist in his poetry.' Discuss in detail the conflict between voice and form in *High Windows*.

3 'The peculiar triumph of Larkin's lyricism is to incorporate other people's words.' Select TWO or THREE poems in which Larkin takes on the voices of others and explain the impact of this on the reader.

4 'The most triumphant of Larkin's poems are about failure and ultimately prefer silence to words.' Comment on the validity of this view in relation to at least THREE poems from *High Windows*.

5 Windows provide a central image throughout *High Windows*. Using at least THREE poems, comment on their significance and their role within the collection as a whole.

6 An interviewer once remarked to Larkin, 'your favourite subjects are failure and weakness'. How far do you agree that 'failure and weakness' are 'favourite subjects' in *High Windows*? In your answer you should EITHER refer to TWO or THREE poems OR range more widely through the collection.

7 Remind yourself of the first poem in *High Windows*, 'To the Sea'. To what extent do you agree with the view that, in terms of subject matter and style, this poem is an appropriate introduction to the whole collection?

8 'Seeing and being seen is one of the central images of *High Windows*.' Comment on the role of such images in TWO or THREE poems in the collection.

9 Larkin's verse may best be described as 'formally informal'. How far do you consider this to be a fair summation of his achievement in *High Windows*? Use TWO or THREE poems to illustrate your response.

10 'For all his cynicism, celebration never lies far beneath the surface.' Comment on how far you believe Larkin's verse to be both cynical and celebratory.

11 Images from the natural world play a significant and varied role in *High Windows*. Comment on the purpose and impact of such images in TWO or THREE poems of your choice.

12 'Larkin is often portrayed as being obsessed with death, but *High Windows* is as much about life as it is about death.' How true do you find this summary of the collection? Select TWO or THREE poems to illustrate your response.

13 Humour, and satirical humour in particular, plays an important role in *High Windows*. Choose TWO or THREE poems and explore the use Larkin makes of humour in this collection.

14 Larkin creates a variety of effects through the titles he chooses for his poems. Choose TWO or THREE poems and explore the effects he achieves.

Sample essays

Below are two sample student essays, both falling within the top mark band. You can judge them against the Assessment Objectives for this text for your exam board and decide on the mark you think each deserves, and why. You will be able to see ways in which each could be improved in terms of content, style and accuracy.

Sample essay 1

'Time is an inescapable force in Larkin's poetry.' Consider the truth of this observation, making specific reference to AT LEAST THREE poems in *High Windows*.

Throughout *High Windows* the reader is constantly faced with the pressing issue of time. Whether it is in the relentless march of the years and their impact upon the human body and mind, as in 'The Building' or 'The Old Fools', the benign cycle of time portrayed in 'The Trees', through the use of significant marker dates (e.g. 'Annus Mirabilis', 'Homage to a Government' and 'Livings I') or in the constant evocation of the passage of minutes, hours and days, Larkin keeps the presence of time and its inevitable motion firmly in the reader's consciousness. It is, for him, a critical means by which we as humans can measure and try to make sense of our existence.

The opening poem of the collection, 'To the Sea', provides an excellent example. It takes as its theme the enduring British tradition of the seaside holiday. The poem deals with time on two levels. In one sense time seems meaningless; the seaside holiday is an ongoing, timeless tradition. With the exception of the transistor radios of stanza 2 the holiday world Larkin presents could come from any period from the Victorian era onwards. The images he presents of colourful bathers, 'children, frilled in white', cards of 'Famous Cricketers', the 'same seaside quack' and the 'white steamer' are recognisable to all and defy a specific location in time. Larkin wishes to create a sense of timeless value, a feeling of security. The nostalgic recreation of this seaside world provides both the poet and the reader with a safe world that has not and does not change in spite of the movement of time. (A similar effect is achieved in 'How Distant', where the image of the girl washing her clothes 'ramifies endlessly'.) Larkin carefully creates a sense of meaningful repetition in the poem. The holiday is 'half an annual pleasure, half a rite', creating the sense that it is a significant marker in the yearly cycle, almost like a religious festival. Similarly, in the final stanza, he points out that those who come here 'yearly' are both 'teaching their children' and 'helping the old'. The repeated trips to the seaside are both a form of education and a bridge between the generations through time.

It is important to note, however, that there is also a sense of time moving in the poem. The transistor radios of stanza 2 have already been observed as a sign of the changes wrought by time, and Larkin seems to exclude willingly from his idealised vision other developments in the typical seaside resort, such as the growth of ubiquitous games arcades, themed pubs and pleasure beaches. The opening lines of the poem physically recreate an act of disengagement with one world and entry into another as the holidaymaker steps over the dividing wall. The sense of dislocation is clearly established as the move 'Brings sharply back something known long before'. This phrase alone indicates the extent to which life away from the seaside has changed. This is further emphasised by the shock he feels at the beginning of stanza 2 that it is 'Still going on, all of it, still going on!' The uncertainty of the children also indicates the different and somehow false nature of the place and its separation from real time, as does the movement of the steamer, which is first 'stuck in the afternoon' and later, without further note, is gone. The reader is left in no doubt that this is, in a sense, a false world, a capsule in time that exists alongside and in spite of the rest of the world, rather than being a true reflection of it.

One of the key issues in 'To the Sea' is the cycle of time, and this is also important elsewhere in the collection. 'The Trees', for example, a poem bursting with the potential of life, traces life's annual cycle in the growth of trees. Money, in the poem of that title, reproaches the persona of the poem 'Quarterly'. The salesman of 'Livings I' follows his repeated cycle of visits, and 'Show Saturday', like 'To the Sea', deals with an enduring British tradition which Larkin fervently wishes to 'always be there'. Broader cycles are also considered in 'Forget What Did', where the meaningless daily cycles of the diary-writer are rejected, brought to an end and superseded by the larger cycles of nature and the heavens.

In many of the poems in *High Windows* Larkin focuses acutely on the markers of time – minutes, hours, days, years and even centuries. In 'Livings III', 'the bells discuss the hour's gradations'. This serves to emphasise the dull and mundane nature of dinner table conversation, but also points out the relentless, steady movement of time. In 'Friday Night in the Royal Station Hotel' the passing of the minutes is a significant and relentless marker, accentuating the loneliness of the place. Other examples of a similar nature are found in 'Sad Steps', 'Money', 'Cut Grass' and 'The Explosion', in all of which the passage of time or specific times of day are important. Time of day is also significant in 'The Building'. Here Larkin sets the patients apart from the rest of (healthy) humanity by the fact that they are in the hospital during the hours of the working day. Larkin also uses larger markers of time, however. In 'Posterity', the biographer Jake Balokowsky complains that he is 'stuck with this old fart at least a year', and 'Forget What Did', 'The Trees', 'Show Saturday' and 'To the Sea' all deal with annual cycles. 'How Distant' goes still further as the poet considers the swift and sudden impact of time's passing in his evocation of 'the startled century'. In 'The Building', the terraced houses surrounding the hospital are 'a great sigh out of the last century', a metaphor serving to emphasise the startling presence of the hospital towering threateningly over surrounding life. And 'The Card-Players' moves to a vision of 'Wet century-wide trees', a vivid temporal image of desolation and darkness. In a similar vein, 'Annus Mirabilis' (in which 1963 becomes a symbolic year of liberation), 'Homage to a Government' and 'Livings I' (the date at the end of the poem is offered as a significant marker, the end of an era, the end of a family tradition) all include specific dated references for the reader as a means of measuring the impact of the issues Larkin is dealing with.

A final key feature of this collection is a repeated sense of an almost spiritual dimension to time. On a number of occasions this is specifically related to death, as in 'Sympathy in White Major', 'The Building', 'The Explosion' and 'The Old Fools'. In these poems the presence of time seems vaguely ridiculous, even insignificant, as humans pathetically attempt to relive, reverse and even recapture time in the face of eternity. In 'Show Saturday', the agricultural show represents something unchanging and unchangeable, which has a profound impact on Larkin. He invokes 'time's rolling smithy-smoke', which 'Shadows much greater gestures', indicating a deeper dimension of time. Such an impression is taken still further in 'High Windows', which traces a line from concrete time to abstract time, paralleling the poem's movement from the bodily to the spiritual. It begins with words such as 'outdated' and 'forty years back' to illustrate the social, religious and sexual changes the poem traces, but concludes with the 'endless', eternal vistas of the skies. 'Solar', similarly, provides an almost cosmic view of time. The sun, like a great heavenly clock (the physical likeness is surely deliberate), benignly measures out our days:

> Our needs hourly
> Climb and return like angels.
> Unclosing like a hand,
> You give for ever.

In *High Windows* Larkin demonstrates his constant awareness of time. As has been identified, however, this operates on a number of different levels. Many of the poems chart the movement of people or objects, opinions or traditions through time. The continual references to markers of time maintain the reader's awareness of the inevitable ticking of the clock, frequently as a countdown through bodily, mental and social decay towards death. However, Larkin is also tempted by temporal visions of the timeless and the eternal, a counter-current within the collection which seems to hold out some kind of deeper meaning and hope within his often bleak portrayal of life.

Sample essay 2

'Larkin is fascinated by the relationship between the individual and society.' Considering AT LEAST THREE poems, explore Larkin's presentation of this relationship in *High Windows*.

The relationship between the individual and society and the related issues of loneliness and isolation are concerns at the heart of Larkin's *High Windows*. In some poems isolation appears as both a positive and a negative force, but elsewhere it is a source only of suffering and of loneliness, an inescapable void which cannot be overcome. Society or community may be seen in two ways; either as the extension (or the opponent) of the individual, or as the opposite of isolation. Both of these play a vital role in *High Windows*. Frequently it is the very presence of others, the proximity of tangible life that most poignantly establishes the presence of isolation, forcing the individual or the group to recognise his or her separation from society. Loneliness and isolation are often at their most destructive and evident in the context of community.

'Vers de Société' is a significant poem. It looks in detail at the relationship between the individual and society and the relative value of each. More specifically it focuses on social gatherings and their impact on the individual explored through the rather jaded eyes of a figure who would evidently prefer to opt out of the round of social events the poem depicts. He desires peaceful isolation from endless people, but feels obliged to be part of the social round. His attitudes are cuttingly displayed at the outset, which juxtaposes the form of polite invitation with abuse:

> My wife and I have asked a crowd of craps
> To come and waste their time and ours: perhaps
> You'd care to join us?

The poem establishes the pervading sense that social intercourse is a waste of time. The vapid chatter of the parties at which this man 'could spend half my evenings' is summed up in 'the drivel of some bitch/Who's read nothing but *Which*'. The trite patter of the rhyme reflects the emptiness of the woman's reading and her conversation. The disillusioned narrator mentally rejects the empty social gatherings and the 'glass of washing sherry' in favour of the forces of meaningful nature – 'the noise of wind' and 'the moon thinned/To an air-sharpened blade'. He is forced, as the poem progresses, to recognise that growing older brings with it the pressure of social demands, the tacit insistence that the individual pay his or her debt to society, the price of which is socialising, summed up in the mantras 'All solitude is selfish' and 'Virtue is social'.

The man then goes on to relate this to broader social changes. The figure of the hermit is significant in this respect, representing a solitary, contemplative and spiritual way of life that 'No one now/Believes'. Instead of the religious beliefs of the hermit, the man, dissatisfied, presents the idea that socialising is the new religion, 'Playing at goodness, like going to church'. To cut himself off like the hermit, however, is too threatening a possibility. Growl under his breath as he might, mock as he does, this man dares not fully disengage himself from the social round as in some strange way this seems to help him define himself. To 'be alone freely', he suggests as the poem ends, is the luxury of the young.

The poem explores a bitter sense of loss of individuality and personality. The ever-pressing demands for social intercourse lead the man to a profound sense of isolation from which he cannot escape even if he truly desired to do so, summed up in the ironic reflection, 'Funny how hard it is to be alone'.

'The Old Fools' and 'The Building' both explore the relationship between the individual and society through the lens of bodily dysfunction, whether because of illness or old age. In 'The Old Fools' Larkin presents us with a blackly humorous and pathetic picture of the elderly, who find themselves increasingly unable to maintain full contact with either their memories or their bodies. As a result of their failing faculties, the aged fall into a new and strange social twilight where they live in a nightmarish dream of imperfectly remembered and imperfectly experienced society. They find themselves more and more divorced from the realities of the present, unable even to summon up a scream of horror at their situation. The 'million-petalled flower of being here' progressively withers as the individual loses the ability to engage in the act of living, and inevitably descends towards death, a lonely experience that happens within but not with the society that surrounds them. However, it is the black irony of the poem that this is a society we shall all join at some point.

'The Building' explores a similar dislocation of the individual from society, dispassionately presenting the fear and loneliness the individual experiences in the face of illness and the failure of the body. These set the patients in the hospital apart from the surrounding world. Larkin clearly separates the patients in the hospital from the people outside, going about their daily business, and from the doctors, nurses and others who work within the hospital, who appear as threatening, almost predatory figures: 'Every few minutes comes a kind of nurse/To fetch someone away'. The presence of the hospital workers and visitors, who are in possession of their health (representatives of conventional society), serves only to point out this contrast more markedly. When they enter the hospital, the patients find 'homes and names/Suddenly in abeyance', as if they become faceless non-beings for the duration of their stay. This is an impression reinforced by his disturbing invocation of 'The unseen congregations whose white rows/Lie set apart above', where the individual has been completely subsumed within a nameless and faceless alternative society of the sick.

As suggested, the hospital represents a strange, alternative society. Larkin describes the building as 'ground curiously neutral' (stanza 3). It is a place (and a society) that makes no distinctions. It is no respecter of class or age or experience. All such societal divisions and distinctions crumble into insignificance the face of this place:

> In it, conceits
> And self-protecting ignorance congeal
> To carry life, collapsing only when
> Called to these corridors

The use of the enjambement here subtly reflects the way in which the patients have been carried over into a new and disturbing alternative reality. The age of the patients is almost irrelevant: 'some are young,/Some old, but most at that vague age that claims/The end of choice', and similarly, Larkin tells us 'women, men;/Old, young' are 'crude facets of the only coin//This place accepts'. Humanity is the payment this place demands for its services,

regardless of colour, creed, gender or age. As in 'Vers de Société' and 'The Old Fools', however, this is a truth that society as a whole chooses to ignore, an uncomfortable reality they exclude until forced, on an individual basis, to face it for themselves in isolation. The loneliness of the experience of illness is emphasised by the nature of the hospital and its society, a place of 'frightening smell[s]', 'confess[ion]' and the end of hope for the sick. It is a place the healthy in society ignore, but will inevitably come to.

'Forget What Did' provides a final useful poem to consider. In this poem the diary-writer (one of a number of social misfits Larkin presents in the collection, including the central figures of 'High Windows' and 'Annus Mirabilis') chooses to stop writing his diary. In so doing he deliberately isolates himself both from his past and from the rest of society. The choice to withdraw himself from the quotidian events of his life inevitably distances him from the people with whom he comes into contact. His chosen isolation links him to the figure of the hermit in 'Vers de Société'. However, where the hermit's choice is based on a positive ideology and the desire to draw nearer to God, in the case of the diary-writer the decision seems more negative. The impact of withdrawal on the individual is profound, summed up in the observation that it is 'a stun to memory'. Unlike the hermit who seeks meaning in God, this man and his diary are now subject to other subsuming powers – nature and the heavens. He opts to remove himself from the painful memories of his past, as if the choice not to write means that the events of his life, 'the wars and winters' of social intercourse, can be 'Hurried to burial' and will cease to be concrete.

Each of these four poems deals closely with the relationship between the individual and wider society. This relationship is complex and ambiguous, simultaneously necessary and painful. Larkin subtly explores the balance between individuals' desires and the wider mores of society, as well as the simultaneous existence of mainstream and alternative societies. The interrelation of these elements is never simple. Larkin recognises the need for all humans both to engage and to withdraw, to belong and to be alone. It is in the exploration of these contrary needs (and the tensions that arise as a result) that Larkin most effectively displays his fascination with the individual and social needs of humanity.

Using the critics

The role of literary criticism and literary theory in the study of literature at both AS and A2 is central. Assessment Objective 4 specifically requires students to 'articulate informed, independent judgements, showing understanding of different interpretations of literary texts by different readers'.

While this does not necessarily mean that all such interpretations should be by established literary critics or propound particular theoretical readings, the implication that these should be covered as part of advanced study is clear, especially where incisive and detailed analysis is required. Furthermore, the emphasis placed on a range of readings makes the use of criticism essential to success.

The following is an extract from the AQA specification, developing some of the implications of Assessment Objective 4:

> Candidates will be expected to show awareness of the following:
> - that, as readers, we are influenced by our own experiences, actual or imagined, and that our cultural background has an effect on our interpretation; thus the interpretation of literary texts, or the determination of their significance, can depend on the interpretative stance taken by the reader
> - that there might be significant differences in the way literary texts are understood in different periods, and by different individuals or social groups
> - that texts do not reflect an external and objective reality; instead they embody attitudes and values
> - that there are different ways of looking at texts, based on particular approaches and theories. Using these theories will require some understanding of critical concepts and terminology
> - that literary texts are frequently open-ended, so ambiguity and uncertainty are central to the reading of texts. Examination tasks will therefore expect candidates to take part in genuine critical enquiry rather than respond to tasks where the teacher/examiner already knows the 'right' answer

You need to think carefully about how critical material should be used. The emphasis in examination specifications is firmly placed upon a candidate's ability to recognise and evaluate the validity of interpretations from a multiplicity of viewpoints. Approaching a text from a single critical perspective, therefore, or prioritising one at the expense of others, is neither desirable nor helpful. Successful students will apply and develop their critical thinking about the set text in the light of a variety of secondary critical texts.

It is essential, however, that students should not see the use of critical quotation as a virtue in its own right. Unthinking application of critical material is at best redundant and at worst prevents students from thinking for themselves. The key to successful application of literary criticism and literary theory is to use it as a basis for argument. There are three basic positions that can be adopted:

(1) To agree with a critical proposition and to use this to support an argument or part of an argument.
(2) To agree with a proposition but with qualifications; identify clearly the areas of agreement, but go on to develop areas of disagreement, qualification, modification or extension of the ideas.
(3) To disagree with a proposition, explaining why.

All of these stances can, of course, be developed by going on to propose alternative critical or theoretical possibilities and evaluating the validity of one critical perspective over another in relation to the text or passage under consideration. To

extend and enrich a response, the criticism used must be engaged with. The words of literary critics and literary theorists should not be taken as received wisdom to be applied unthinkingly to the text. Instead, you need to identify clearly the issues raised by the critic and then evaluate and test these in relation to the set text, which should always remain the primary focus of your response.

References and further study

Larkin's main works

Poetry

The North Ship (1945)
XX Poems (1951)
The Fantasy Poets No. 21 (1954)
Poems (1954)
The Less Deceived (1955)
The Whitsun Weddings (1964)
High Windows (1974)
Collected Poems 1938–83 (1988)

Fiction

Jill (1946)
A Girl in Winter (1947)
Trouble at Willow Gable and Other Fictions (2002)

Non-fiction

Larkin, P. (1970) *All What Jazz: A Record Diary 1961–71*, Faber and Faber.
Larkin, P. (1983) *Required Writing: Miscellaneous Pieces 1955–82*, Faber and Faber.
Palmer, R. and White, J. (eds) (2001) Larkin's Jazz: Essays and Reviews 1940–84, Continuum.
Thwaite, A. (ed.) (1982) *Larkin at Sixty*, Faber and Faber.
Thwaite, A. (ed.) (1992) *Selected Letters of Philip Larkin 1940–85*, Faber and Faber.
Thwaite, A. (ed.) (2001) *Further Requirements: Interviews, Broadcasts, Statements and Reviews, 1952–85*, Faber and Faber.

Biography

Motion, A. (1993) *Philip Larkin: A Writer's Life*, Faber and Faber.

Literary criticism

Morrison, B. (1980) *The Movement: English Poetry and Fiction of the 1950s*, Oxford University Press.
Rossen, J. (1989) *Philip Larkin: His Life's Work*, Harvester Wheatsheaf.

Swarbrick, A. (1995) *Out of Reach: Poetry of Philip Larkin*, Macmillan.

Thwaite, A. (1970) 'The Poetry of Philip Larkin' in *Survival of Poetry: A Contemporary Survey*, ed. M. Dodsworth, Faber and Faber.

Websites

www.literaryhistory.com/20thC/Larkin.htm

www.philiplarkin.com

www.poets.org/poet.php/prmPID/176

www.todayinliterature.com/biography/philip.larkin.asp

www.infoplease.com/ce6/people/A0828895.html

www.litencyc.com/php/speople.php?rec=true&UID=2624